In Practice

Moving Beyond Law School Theory

This book is for all the young lawyers who eagerly attack their studies, only to find out that they have to start from scratch once they hit the profession.

WHAT'S INSIDE?

PART ONE
THE STUFF AT THE START

INTRODUCTION

It isn't often that we get a good look into the one on one discussions between a senior lawyer and their protégé. Normally such relationships are kept private and secretive, and we rarely get insight into what goes on.

However, with this collection I have managed to pull together a valuable look into the mentoring relationship and the training provided to a young lawyer by a very senior partner.

What is it that we are looking at, exactly?

An aspiring young lawyer, Thomas, has chosen to embark upon a legal career. His family has a long and illustrious history of legal practice, and are keen to see Thomas' career take off in the direction that they think is most appropriate.

As a result, his well-meaning (but occasionally overbearing) uncle Andrew has taken it upon himself to instruct Thomas in the ways of legal practice. Andrew manages to find a significant amount of time to spend writing to Thomas, to ensure that Thomas is on the right track.

Despite my search I have located only one side of the dialogue here. While we are fortunate to have Andrew's correspondence to his nephew, we do not have the benefit of Thomas' responses.

I hope that you enjoy this insight into the real world of legal practice. Take from it what you will. I, of course, do not express a view about Andrew's training methods nor about his opinions – they are merely what they are, and you will have to decide for yourself what truth there is in his instruction.

For my part I think Andrew can teach us a lot. Whether or not you agree with Andrew is irrelevant – it is through turning your mind to the issues he raises that you are most likely to benefit from his letters.

A Note on Editing

In the process of getting these manuscripts into a usable form for you, I have added some formatting and punctuation. It seems Uncle Andrew put his own drafting advice to good use, and commonplace mechanisms to allow easy reading of his letters (like paragraphs, for example) were not included in the originals. For the sake of your eyes I have remedied these.

Naturally if there are any errors in spelling, grammar or punctuation - I will gladly land those directly at Andrew's feet.

Happy Lawyering!

Chris

How to Use this Book

Okay so I accept it's a little unusual to have a "how to use this book" section in what is really a set of fictional letters.

This book, however, is not just a pleasant aside in which I dig into the world of legal practice for your temporary amusement. It's not designed to be read and forgotten.

Instead, this book is designed to provoke you.

Specifically, it is designed to provoke your thoughts about what kind of lawyer you want to be, and what kind of practice you want to have.

As you will see, I run through any number of day to day practical issues that you are going to face, in a form that I intend to be approachable and useful.

So you could just read this as a vaguely amusing treatise on modern legal practice.

Or you could use it to help you define yourself, to help you think about what actually matters and what doesn't, and to help you discern how you are going to approach **your** legal career.

As you read, think about this: have you considered the issues that are raised? Just how far have you taken that thought?

Have you thought about career progression, and whether you are on the default path that's been provided for you, or one of your choosing?

Have you contemplated your practice areas, your networking strategies, your marketing? Have you been pushed in one direction because "that's just how it's done" or did you choose it yourself? Have you considered what style of writing you want to develop, and how you want to approach your work/life balance (if there is such a thing)?

What about building a team? Before long you'll need to manage staff, deal with internal conflict and get the best out of people - can you do that? Have you even thought about what that involves?

Those are the real world subjects of this book, and they are designed to get you thinking.

Use them to your advantage and take the opportunity to start defining yourself as a legal practitioner.

FREE COURSES TO HELP

On its own, you will hopefully find this book a slightly different approach to teaching you about some important aspects of legal practice. It is designed to get you to think, to engage, and to actively consider what really matters in your own practice as you journey through your legal career.

However, I know that some of you will want to take it further, and I can offer you that opportunity.

Therefore, I wanted to point you in the direction of some free courses in legal skills that you start today.

If you're serious about your legal career and you want to experience a true growth in your legal skills, then I encourage you to explore one, two or all of the courses available.

You can find them at:

- Learning Hub: http://www.tipsforlawyers.com/learn
- Legal Drafting: http://www.tipsforlawyers.com/legal-writing-course
- Wellness: http://www.tipsforlawyers.com/wellness
- Networking and Marketing: http://www.tipsforlawyers.com/networking
- Professional Habits: http://www.tipsforlawyers.com/habits

PART TWO
You've Decided to Study Law... Seriously?

So You're Studying Law

My Dear Nephew Thomas,

I have heard from your parents that you have now commenced your legal studies.

Unfortunately I am, at present, very busy in my own practice and cannot write to you at length. However I shall watch your progress with great interest, and look forward to hearing about your excellent grades and various successes.

For myself, I might say that the law has been a rewarding and fulfilling career, and when you hit your stride in the real world after finishing your studies, I hope that it will be for you also.

As you know, our (your) family is an accomplished one when it comes to legal careers – but I shall write to you more about what that means for you another time.

In your studies can I encourage you to ensure that your every waking hour is devoted to the learning of the law? That is, of course, what University is for. It is unlikely that your University (prestigious though it may be) will teach you anything that will allow you to practise law, but we can work on those skills together as you need them.

It would be useful when we get to that point if I do not have to explain fundamental legal principles to you - it would slow both you and I down.

For now, just know that you have my support and encouragement, and I look forward to hearing from you.

Yours faithfully,

Andrew Berringer

Senior Partner – Berringer, Riddle and McCarthew

Are your Marks Good Enough?

Dear Thomas,

I thought I would take a moment and see how you were travelling in your studies?

For the time being, I remain ensconced in legal practice, but I hope that my occasional notes so far have been useful for you, or at least mildly interesting in terms of the things to come.

For the moment, I was wondering how your grades were going?

Given the length of time since I myself studied my Bachelor of Laws, I will not presume to instruct you on the best way to achieve superior results. Suffice it to say that your focus should be on utilising whatever method seems most qualified to provide you with a good academic outcome.

That said, there is a habit among young aspiring lawyers which seems to require them to drink heavily and party a lot during their studies.

They then complain that they have insufficient time to study, and insufficient time to prepare their assignments and assessment tasks (they also complain of a lack of funds, which I find especially amusing given the number of dollars handed over in exchange for continuous inebriation).

I am sure that, presented in this way, you can immediately see the irony of these two positions? A young person who devotes themselves to drinking and partying will, necessarily, have insufficient time to devote themselves to the study of law.

This is not a permanent state. As you will see, the ability to socialise and drink with others is, in fact, an important skill to cultivate. It is not, however, presently a concern of yours and you should be absolutely focused on making the most of the considerable investment that your parents have made in your career by sending you to what is arguably the best University in the country.

I am reliably informed that you have more than sufficient mental faculties at your disposal to do extremely well in your studies. So really the only question you need to ask yourself is: are you prepared to put in the work that is required to achieve top grades?

I look forward, as always, to hearing about your progress.

Best Regards,

Uncle Andrew

YOUR FINAL YEAR

[Editor's note – although I believe that Andrew wrote to his nephew from time to time during the period of his studies, I have not been able to locate many of those other letters – presumably the state of Thomas' college accommodation did not allow for the careful protection of paperwork]

Dear Thomas,

It seems only yesterday that you had commenced your studies and started the ridiculous subject called "introduction to law" - as if by calling it that they could somehow achieve it - and yet here we find ourselves, with your graduation imminent.

That said, it has been comforting to see that your results have not slipped as time went on, as they do with some many eager young lawyers to be, who hit their initial subjects with enthusiasm and then find themselves stumped when it comes to the world of Constitutional Law or Equitable Doctrine.

It has been pleasant writing to you these years, although I would have preferred a more frequent response from you. I can only assume that your time in study and other beneficial activities has kept you appropriately occupied.

Upon completion of your tertiary subjects and after your graduation, I imagine that to become a "real" lawyer you will now be expected to complete the modern day version of Articles of Clerkship, called "Practical Legal Training".

It is a course which is, regrettably, inferior in every way to the training which I enjoyed under my master when at a similar age.

However, complete it you must and in these times I have started to take a more sanguine approach to such things, knowing as I do that any young lawyer or graduate who wishes to learn the actual practice of law will find for themselves an accessible lawyer from whom they can learn.

I acknowledge, of course, the possible (but unlikely) chance that the course you embark upon will offer some actual benefit to you.

Please know that there is no substitute for the training that I had from my master, and I would strongly suggest that you acquire one of your own, whether mandated by your local legal association or not. Your master will provide you with something that no sanitised education can – the real world perspective.

I expect that you will find it old fashioned and laughable to call such a person your "master" and so you need not do so, of course, but that is what they are and that is how I will refer to them.

The real world is very different from the institution driven training you will receive. You probably already know this intuitively, but you do not necessarily know it with specificity. What the real world brings into the equation is the **context** of legal practice. There is no comparison between a sanitised set of facts designed to give you a chance to tell (or write down) everything you know about contract law, and a client screaming down the phone at you for an answer on the spot in a "yes or no" form before they commit to a costly decision.

So while I support necessary training, I do not support it in isolation of real world matters that you must learn if you are to survive. The ability to prepare work under pressure, to deal with irrational stress created by clients, and to understand the effect of your decisions on profit – these are the things that you must learn if you are going to succeed.

So get a master.

On another note, I find myself in a position where more of my time may become available soon. Happily that may coincide with your graduation and admission to the profession, and so with your permission I will speak with your parents about my continued involvement in your practice.

Yours faithfully,

Andrew Berringer

Consultant – Berringer, Riddle and McCarthew

Articles (Practical Legal Training)

Dear Thomas,

I gather you are finding your experience of Practical Legal Training tedious and cumbersome?

I am not too surprised, and so I sympathise with your situation. Although my brothers in the profession who formulate these courses do so with the best of intentions, it is quite apparent that the curriculum becomes polluted with the interests of academics and various pencil pushers who have probably never practised law, let alone met with a client or entered a Courtroom.

The result is that the course you presently undertake represents, at best, an extension of your University education. It is primarily academic, although seeks to provide you with some practical expertise so that you might not be completely useless to your employers (once you have an employer, that is).

Although I have touched on it previously, there are a number of distinguishing features between actual legal work and what you now do that I thought I would highlight, lest you subconsciously start to think that your current sanitised situation could represent what you have to look forward to.

The first primary difference is money. The fictitious clients in your course almost never call you up about your fee estimates (which you almost never have to provide them). They appear to have the ability and the will to "fight on principle" or some such nonsense.

You are never forced to account for the competing interests of the client's immediate requirements which might not align with your firm's requirement for you to get funds in your trust account before commencing anything. At no time do you have to confront and solve a client complaint regarding their bill, or confess to a partner that you spent 3 hours longer than was required on a job because you couldn't get the client to shut up on the phone.

These are the realities of practice. Everything you do has to be guided by the fact that your firm needs to make money. If it doesn't make money, then you are out of the job (one way or another). Personally I don't think that's greedy, like some people seem to think. Rather, it's just pragmatism.

The next primary difference is the lack of marketing. In "training land", your work simply flows in and you do it. In the real world, someone has had to fight to get that work in competition with a thousand other practitioners, many of whom cost less and are frequently just as competent (although not always).

There is no qualm about telling your fictitious clients that they have no case, because they won't call your supervising partner who is friends with their mother's brother's cousin, and abuse you to them telling them how incompetent you are while, back at the office, you are forced to defend a perfectly sound legal finding to your now irate partner. These relationship factors are absent in your training.

Next is the nature of facts. In your world at the moment, you get the facts and assume their completeness and accuracy. In the real world, you never get all the facts, and are frequently required to drag them out into the light for examination. Situations change, answers change, documents reveal inconsistencies, and the list goes on. The practice of law is a moving feast, and any given matter might change from a gnat to a dragonfly to an elephant over the span of its existence.

Finally there is the pressure of time. Yes, your assignments have deadlines and due dates. But, within that confine, you can spend as much time as you wish on a particular project. You will not find that situation in law. What you will find is that a task will be required to be completed within an hour, and if you spend more than that you will have to account for it in some way. You will also find that just because you are finished, doesn't meant the job is done. You need to factor in review, settlement, revision, and of course the time that the support staff "do mail" which, if missed, will result in an otherwise unnecessary walk to the post box.

Oh yes - I should mention the paper. There is lots, and lots, of paper that needs to be printed, sorted, filed and dealt with in some way.

These are but some of the many differences which I wanted to highlight in brief to you now, so your brain does not accept the fiction that is presented to you now. Over time you will start to identify more discrepancies for yourself, and no doubt we will discuss them further.

So, while you complete this "practical" course I would like to remind you, again, of the need for you to seek and retain a master who can more effectively guide you in the practicalities of the legal world than the course you now undertake could ever do.

If you are to be effective as a lawyer from day one, you will need to take your education far beyond what you now learn. I encourage you (again) to do so as soon as possible.

Yours faithfully,

Uncle Andrew

PART THREE
OK Fine, If You're Going to be a Lawyer Then...

Welcome to the Profession

My Dear Thomas,

I am informed by your father and mother that you have, finally, completed the course laughably entitled "practical legal training", resulting in your admission to the legal profession. I also believe that you have found yourself employment at a respectable firm.

I would like to congratulate you on that accomplishment, and take a few moments to talk about the times to come.

As you know by now, our family is full of senior solicitors, barristers and judges all around the country. I mention this not to fill you with some kind of false pride in your genetic heritage, but to ensure that you are aware of the (fairly reasonable) expectations that there will be upon you to continue that long and illustrious history.

Given our correspondence throughout your training, your family has taken the view that we should continue the relationship we have begun. To that end, your parents have asked me to be your guardian (mentor, if you will - I've used the word "master" previously but I understand you found it silly) in the legal profession, to ensure that you are getting the lessons you require to excel in, improve at, and ultimately master the necessary legal skills that have elevated our family to our present position.

I expect that you will find my letters of significant assistance - especially since you are not paying for this service I am providing. However, I did want to ensure that I set down some rules for you to follow from the outset of this more formal part of our correspondence, in case you think that I am spending my valuable time in this exercise only as an opportunity for you to do some light reading, put my letters to one side, and then go about your own business with no regard for my input.

The first rule is this: I expect you to put into action all of the advice I give you in these letters. I am well aware (and have mentioned before) that the current mode of studying will have likely imbued you with some significant sense of self-worth, and that you will almost certainly think more of your own abilities than you ought.

In case there is any doubt, from the perspective of myself, your parents, and the other members of our family - you do not know anything. This may sound cruel, but I say it only to ensure that you take to heart my advice, rather than considering yourself to be lacking any need for such things.

Second, I expect you to report back to me in a timely fashion each week your activities for the preceding period. There is no need to tell me about your non-professional activities. My focus is, as you must know by this point, upon your legal development and success. Your reports ought to be at least 2 pages in length, and handwritten.

You may feel inclined on occasion to send me an "email" – I suggest you fight that temptation. Not only am I unlikely to read it (or, for that matter, locate my email address) but I find email to be a ridiculous form of communication suitable only for the exchange of such pleasantries as "are you coming over for dinner tonight?" and the like. It is not, however, appropriate for the expression of any complex thought nor for the delivery of reports like those which I will be asking you to send me.

From the reports you deliver I will, of course, tailor my advice to ensure that I am delivering to you information that is valuable to your immediate circumstances. What I am really saying is this: the quality of my suggestions and advice for you will be determined by the quality of your reports to me.

Finally (and I cannot stress this enough) unless we agree otherwise, your correspondence to me is not confidential and you should not expect it to be.

As I have mentioned already, you carry with you a significant burden to ensure the continued success of this family, so you can expect that your professional development will be a matter of interest to all of us. That said, sometimes I will ask that you keep my comments private to yourself. There are some truths in the profession that seem to be politically incorrect to say aloud, and while I will be honest with you about those I don't think either of us will make any friends through their publication.

With those ground rules in place, I will conclude this letter.

Please ensure you deliver to me your first report on your activities and experiences within 7 days of starting your position.

Your Humble Servant,

Uncle Andrew

BEGINNING YOUR LESSONS

Dear Thomas,

As a bit more of a primer to our relationship, I thought it would be appropriate to let you know where we were headed from here.

You see, in your studies and your legal training so far, the reality is that you have had your head stuffed with a number of untruths.

Part of my role as your guide through the profession is going to be to remedy some of those misconceptions, as I have already started to do.

The first and most obvious deficiency is that you have learnt only law (and I assure you it is a drop in the ocean). However, the learning of the law by itself is not an acceptable form of preparation for legal practice. Even within your "practical" training course, you have been met with an approach that is fundamentally different to that which you find in practice. You have hypothetical situations which are sanitised, conditioned and cleansed to give rise to a specific occasion.

You will find none of this in legal practice. I have, of course, written to you about that before and have already set out a few examples for you.

Knowledge is only part of the picture. Knowledge alone will not give you a career. It will not bring you clients nor endear you to your employers. Knowledge cannot tell you how to respond to an angry client, nor to arrange for an increase in your salary. In short: knowledge is not all you need.

You can see the blanks that begin to appear. In days past, many of these needs would have been met by your articles of clerkship, but no longer. I accept that there are many who did not appreciate their clerkship, suffering as they did at the hands of the incompetent, the bully or the disengaged master.

But you are fortunate to have a family that cares about your career and which is prepared to invest in you so that you might rise swiftly within your firm. That is where my guidance will come in.

I do not intend to teach you the law, for a number of reasons. The first is that I am ill-equipped. I do not know where you might find yourself, and in my retirement I have no intention of keeping pace with changes in legal technicalities in the same way you will have to day to day. The next is that you already know the law; or at least, you already know where to find the law. Should it be required you can research, read, learn, distill and explain it all by yourself. My assistance there is hardly necessary.

What I do intend to teach you is how to be a lawyer.

It is a complex task to teach, and a complex lesson to learn. There are some who might say that you will learn to be a lawyer through simply being one - no extra effort on our part being required (in short - that specific and dedicated mentoring in the legal profession is a waste). And there is truth in the proposition that you will improve over time, but beneath the surface of the statement there are a number of problems.

You will already be aware of the fierce competition that you now face with your peers. Compared to the time when I commenced my career, the numbers of students and young lawyers in comparison to the overall profession is staggering. There is a dramatic oversupply of students.

I am sure you like to think that your talents and existing connections will let you rise to the top, but you cannot assume that. Most young law students are smart, eager, and disciplined to some extent. They share many common characteristics due to their similar training, have similar knowledge and have similar goals and aspirations. So what makes you so special? Those who have the benefit of a mentor like you do have an immediate benefit. Having a source of knowledge and assistance greater than the others around you will serve you in potentially dramatic ways.

The next reason that "learning as you go" is inadequate is because of its ponderous pace. Again related to the numbers in the profession these days, you will find that your advancement will be significantly slower than that of the generation before you, or the one before them. I expect you will find that fairly annoying, and rightly so. However, it is simply a function of current economics. Part of my role is to help you navigate your career advancement in a way that out paces those around you. If I can do that, you will reach your goals faster and, as a result, have a much more satisfying and lucrative career.

Finally, it is not just a matter of pace and competition - it is a matter of being better. Tell yourself whatever you want, but I have been a lawyer for more than 40 years, and you have not.

That means that I know what I am doing. I am successful and you are not (yet). There are many lawyers my age who have not had the success that I have. If you pay attention, apply yourself and engage with my teaching properly - you will simply do better.

So what do we have? We have you rising above the competition. We have you doing it faster. And we have you doing it better. Does that sound like something you might want to do?

I thought so.

We'll get into just how you can do that shortly. But first, perhaps a little taste of what you're going to learn (unless your feedback requires specific attention in any particular area, of course).

First I'm going to spend some time writing to you about the mental state you need to be an effective lawyer. We're going to talk about how you should approach work, how you should approach promotion, and some mental and practical strategies designed to ensure that you are framing your mindset correctly to be a good lawyer.

Once you are ready for it, I'm going to start talking about marketing and networking. Obviously you need to have clients, or you're not going to ever be a partner. We'll talk about building your network, and we'll talk about building your practice.

If you have those mastered, we will start to talk about making money - how law firms do it, how you can improve it, and how you can start to participate in the profits. We're also going to talk about dealing with your team to get the best out of them.

If you manage to grasp those things and master them through implementation then you will be successful, as I have been.

I am looking forward to it - I hope that you are as well.

Best regards,

Uncle Andrew

A NOTE ABOUT YOUR WORK HABITS

My Dear Thomas,

Thank you for delivering your written, if brief, report on your activities to me. Another day I might write to you about the use of the English language, and how you might go about applying it to your reports instead of using whatever it was that you were endeavouring to use in your letter.

For now, however, I wanted to draw your attention to an immediate problem in your career that, if allowed to continue unchecked, is likely to ruin you from the beginning. It is the issue of your work hours.

I see that the firm you have started with has encouraged you to leave "right on 5:00pm" as if, somehow, they are doing you a favour in making that suggestion.

You have further indicated that this is the situation because "at first" you will not likely have too much work to do until they have built up your workload.

Whatever benevolent reason your firm may have for this directive, it is misconceived. It is well known to me and your parents that the lawyers who advance the fastest are those who spend the most time in the office.

Here is what is happening when you leave at 5:00pm as invited: everybody else is still there. And so, on the one hand, we have those around you who are seen to be busy, productive, and present in the office at all times. They are available for the inevitable urgent calls that come in after hours, and when the senior partners walk around the office towards the end of the day, they will see who is there.

And what will they see when they get to your desk? Nothing.

They will not see you, because you are not there. In fact, not only will they not see you but they will likely never even realise who you are. If you were in charge of the allocation of complex work or decisions regarding promotions, ask yourself this: would you promote somebody that you couldn't identify? Of course not.

Instead, promotions and quality work will be given out to those who are studiously at their desks or actively in the office at all hours of the day.

You will inevitably suggest that the lack of work at the present time is somehow connected to your early departure from the office. That is, of course, irrelevant.

So that you are not deceived, you may take the truth as this: you must be present in the office for at least as many hours a day as the senior partners in your firm are. Your lack of work to do makes no difference. If you need to occupy yourself with what has become known as "busy work" then you should do so. If need be you can ultimately replace that with actual work, but really it doesn't matter for the purposes of achieving our particular goal at this time. The point of the exercise is not that you are actually **doing** anything so much as it is that you are **seen** to be working hard in the office.

Since we have started on the concept of capacity for work, however, you should also remember that when asked about your capacity for work, you must always indicate that you are quite busy, but could take on a little more.

Do not stop to consider the precise accuracy of the statement in a given situation. The point is not to be precise in your answer, but to make it clear that first, you are in demand and therefore busy, but next that you are able to provide more value through taking on additional tasks if required.

The statement is, of course, subjective and therefore it is not untruthful in any given circumstances, in case you were concerned about that.

For these reasons you may politely discard the "invitation" to leave at 5:00pm. Your presence in the office is important.

As a final note, in researching the firm in which you now find yourself and the issue that I have addressed in this letter, I have noticed that they promote themselves as having "work/life balance".

That phrase is, of course, a polite fiction. A perfectly civil and politically correct one, to be sure. Indeed if the firm did not promote their working conditions using that description, they would find themselves isolated from the greater legal community as perhaps the only firm in the country who did not do so.

This is where you need to carefully consider what is being put forward here. "Work/life balance" is a phrase which has no identifiable meaning.

Picture some scales, if you can (the kind your grandmother uses with a fulcrum in the middle and balanced weights on either side). All "work/life balance" means is that both sides of the scales are even. Now this can be achieved in a number of ways. Think of your work as a large weight on the one side. Then picture 50 other, much smaller, weights. It is those which sit on the other side, balancing out the scales against your work.

And that is how it is with the "work/life" balance that your firm promotes, and you should adopt. The "work" component forms, of itself, a disproportionate weight towards how you should be allocating your time.

The balance of your activities, when added together, will ultimately take a similar proportion of your time and energy. However, work is the predominate factor in your life, and given how long your career will be you had best get used to thinking that way now.

I look forward to your next report. If you would confirm that you have understood my points about office hours, I would be obliged.

Yours in retirement,

Uncle Andrew.

THE CORPORATE LADDER

Dear Thomas,

It is most gratifying to read of, and hear from my friends about, your extended and more appropriate work hours. I take it my previous advice has not gone unheeded, and you are now starting to see some of the benefits of being present in the office.

With some of your new and much improved habits in the office now well underway, I wanted to take a moment to discuss your future.

It is true that, as it stands, you are quite unimportant (not to me personally, you understand, but in an economic sense to your firm). Your contributions to the bottom line are almost non-existent, and I am sure that your various partners' time is presently being spent fixing mistakes that everyone wishes you would not make.

Sometimes I do think to myself that junior lawyers are, in fact, almost entirely responsible for the ongoing survival of the red pen industry, for surely there is no other single contributor to the need for red ink as a draft document that has been produced by a junior lawyer.

Your work habits notwithstanding, it is important that you

understand a little more about how you are most likely to be promoted in your firm.

You should not expect assistance from us (that is, your parents and I) in this, because it would be inappropriate for us to intervene in your career in a direct way. However, what we can do is ensure that you have the benefit of our advice which, as you know, comes with the most important pedigree of all: we have done it before.

No doubt you have heard along the way from naive professors and teachers of law that if you "work hard" and "apply yourself" you will advance in your firm. This is poppycock.

There are two factors, and two alone, that are relevant to your advancement in your firm.

First comes billing. I don't care how much law anybody knows – if they are not billing their time to make me enough money, then not only am I (should I still be the managing partner, and not retired) likely to disregard their name for important matters and promotions, I am almost certainly likely to fire them.

I can hear your protest already in my ears – you are thinking "but Uncle Andrew, they are not giving me enough work to do, how can I possibly bill more time". Such is the initial response of all new lawyers, and so I do understand. This is one of the major areas where your education has failed to properly equip you, and a large part of the reason that I find myself in these communications with you.

For the moment, I accept that you cannot generate work out of thin air, and that the kind of work you are doing is likely to be a little piecemeal in nature. The result is that you might struggle to fill your days if you are working too quickly.

Did you notice how I said "too quickly"? Well that is, in fact, the key to the issue. On a given day, let us say you are trying to bill no less than 8 billable hours that day (a modest number, but appropriate for a person as junior as you – in time you will easily achieve 14 billable hours a day whilst working only 10, a matter that we can discuss at a later date and which is likely not an appropriate subject to be reduced to writing).

What you, in your tender years, must cultivate is an ability to ensure that the tasks which you have been allotted for the day take, in fact, that entire day. In that way you can make sure that you are billing sufficiently whilst also staying "busy" as I have promoted previously.

There will be occasional murmurings within your firm about how work should be done efficiently and as cost effectively for the client as possible. Rest assured those are merely the vocal outworking of the firm's desire to avoid criticism. That way, if asked, they can honestly answer any question by identifying a "policy" or 'practice manual" where efficiencies are encouraged. Behind closed doors, of course, your superior numbers will quickly bring you to the attention of the right people, for the right reasons.

That leads us nicely to the second element of getting a promotion: being "tight" with the boss. The word on the grapevine is that your boss is a fan of rugby, and has a particular favourite team (I'm sure you know what it is). Guess what? You just became a fan of rugby. I imagine you can figure out which team it is that you follow... Congratulations on having a new and professionally useful hobby. You may now find yourself attending games at which you happen to bump into your boss. Say hello.

Then, of course, the next day you can also happen to see your boss whereupon you will be able to discuss the game and agree with whatever it is that is said to you with wholehearted vigour.

I understand from your mother that your preferred game is the more sedentary chess (or possibly computer games), but unfortunately despite my best efforts I have been unable to locate any of your senior partners who share your interest. I'm afraid you will have to continue to play that one on your own time, because it offers little in the way of professional advancement (at least, for now).

I'm not suggesting falsehood here, of course – I'm suggesting that you genuinely develop a love of rugby, and quickly.

Be careful, however, because I (and everybody else I know who cares to have an opinion about such things) abhor people trying to get my attention only for their own benefit. If you are perceived as a "suck up" it will likely do more damage to your career than good.

No, what you are looking for is opportunities to interact about areas of common (or soon to be common) interest.

That, combined with your excellent billing habits will set you well on your way.

I look forward to hearing of your advancement soon.

Yours in eager anticipation,

Andrew

PS –you might put slightly more effort into your penmanship. I recognise that with the advent of the computer such disposables as "ink" have become otiose, but since we are corresponding in this far more civilised manner, how about you take the opportunity to improve your script in order that I need not have it decoded by a cryptographer before next responding. Perhaps acquire a decent pen?

IMPROVE YOUR LETTER WRITING

Thomas,

I see that my polite suggestion for you to develop decipherable handwriting must have slipped your mind.

Your latest update is, I regret to say, completely illegible. What few words I managed to make out suggest that you have decided not to take this relationship as seriously as you ought.

I felt it time to give you some useful instruction in the area of letter writing. It is clear (from the 10% of your correspondence that I can actually read) that your ability to string more than 3 monosyllabic words together is severely limited.

I have a number of pointers for you that I suggest you take on board and implement in your future correspondence, both with me and others (so I can see how you are improving).

Numerous young people over recent times have suggested to me that my tone, language, and style is inappropriate for people trying to engage in "plain English drafting".

Needless to say, those bright young sparks did not work for me long, and have no doubt gone on to work only for themselves, barely making ends meet and unlikely to succeed in any meaningful way.

Why, you ask, would I make such a harsh assessment of their prospects? The reason is simple – they don't understand the purpose of the written word. The ability to write is, when wielded appropriately, the most powerful tool in a lawyer's arsenal.

In order to ensure that you learn to use this weapon appropriately, I need to impress upon you the untruth of various claims being made by modern day legal writers, none of whom I socialise with and all of whom need to stick to their libraries rather than expressing ignorant opinions about actual legal practice.

Principally you need to remember the point of the document you are writing. Of course at a primary level, your job is still to advise and assist your client.

But the successful lawyer knows how to ensure that their client understands just enough of what is going on to ensure that they are giving you the instructions that you have decided they should give. Beyond that, you need to be careful about making everything too easy to understand.

If clients develop a perception that they, if they turned their mind to it, could actually start to run things themselves, then that is going to create all sorts of unnecessary problems for you.

Indeed, clients these days believe that because they have

access to information they have some kind of entitlement to question decisions and recommendations provided by their lawyers. It is quite irritating, to say the least, and the way you communicate with them can impact on whether they think it is appropriate or not.

No, the trick is to ensure that they understand just enough to **feel** like they are in control of the situation, but not so much they will ever be in a position to criticise your work.

As to your opponents, they will (of course) generally not be subject to the same levels of ignorance about legal matters as your clients.

However, there will be a number of your peers who will write in a style that could cause people to question whether they are really as smart as they put themselves out as being.

Ensuring that you write with an appropriately broad and sophisticated use of language will ensure that your opponents are kept on their guard (unless, of course, you are deliberately trying to achieve something different for strategic purposes).

So with those fundamental points, I should make a further comment about this concept of "plain English drafting", which is essentially the only purported lesson about legal drafting that anyone gets in University these days.

At its most fundamental, the principle seems to refer to a strategic way of making yourself look dumber. Use shorter words, clipped sentences and unsophisticated prose.

To the extent it seeks to do that, I simply cannot understand it. After all, why should the highly educated start catering to the lowest common denominator?

I can understand the modern use of things like "bullet" points and the like, and I do admit that some contracts and legal documents seem to be less of an eye sore these days, but the part of this concept that I fundamentally object to is the idea that we should pretend we are plain spoken when, in most cases, we are not.

I feel it is insulting and, frankly, time wasting to take the necessary amount of additional effort to put something in "plain" language when it is already expressed perfectly well.

After all, it is well known in the profession that most clients are going to simply call you and ask you what your advice means anyway - so why bother making it so easy for them to read when their fundamental laziness is going to mean that they don't read your hard work either way?

So far as it is up to you then, I encourage you not to dumb down your language, your style, and your tone simply for the sake of catering to the unwashed masses.

Enough literary damage has already been done to you during your education, so we can try at this point to stem the tide going forward.

I look forward to reading your improved work soon.

Best regards,

Uncle Andrew

The End Before the Beginning

Dear Thomas,

Among the many targets you will have to set during your legal career, I wonder whether you have turned you mind to the last one?

What do I mean?

When you travel, I'll wager that you spend a great deal of time thinking about what your destination will be like, don't you? You know that on the one hand you have to get your documents, pack your bags, and arrange accommodation - but the inspiration and the energy to do those things come from thinking about your destination and how pleasurable it is going to be.

For you, as for most of us, the end is almost certainly going to be a senior partnership position within a firm. That is the natural conclusion of most engaged in legal practice. Of course, some will take other options, but that is a matter for them.

Why should you turn your mind to the end, particularly at this early stage? One reason is to keep you focused. Having your mind on the end will let you stay on target when it comes to your decisions, your strategies, and your tactics during the course of your career.

The next reason is to ensure that you stay positive. Despite the current trend to say otherwise, I expect your experience is the same as mine: your sense of satisfaction with your profession is going to improve as you become more successful. Presumably you want to increase in status, recognition, power or wealth (or perhaps all of them). As you do those things, you will find two results - first you will feel more accomplished; next, you will want to do it even more. It is a type of virtuous spiral.

Most importantly, however, as you tick off all of these goals, your general feeling of fulfilment will increase.

Take me as an example: prior to my departure from the profession, I was one of the most senior lawyers at a prestigious law firm. I earned a significant income and have powerful and influential friends (some of whom would suggest that I, too, am both powerful and influential).

That achievement caused me significant satisfaction. It was the goal of my youth, then my middle years, to achieve those things - and I did.

In the meantime, I was hungry for more of everything: responsibility, authority, wealth, power, influence.

That hunger is what kept me going through the more difficult times of legal practice (more on difficult times later, that is not the point of this letter). So then, for you this is the question:

what does the end look like to you? What will you have when you "make it" in your career?

I have given you a description of my life alone - you are yourself, and your picture will be different. I've explained to you already what kind of life a lawyer is going to lead, and what the point of a legal career is from my perspective. I expect that you share similar goals for your own, but the process of mapping it in your own mind is important.

So for your next report - describe the end to me. Who will you be, what will you have, and what will you have done?

Before signing off today, however, I did want to elaborate on the topic in a little more detail. I feel that many people misunderstand the process of visualisation, because they do not take the time to explore it properly. There is a trick that your brain will play on you, and I want to ensure that you are aware of it so you do not get caught by it.

Picturing what you want is no new topic, Thomas - in fact the idea has been around now for a long time. But it has become skewed in terms of what it can accomplish. Many people confuse it with goal setting, where they think that by visualising their end result in this way they are somehow setting goals.

Obviously that is not the case. Keeping your end game in mind is no more setting a goal than a dog sets a goal by salivating at the thought of a bone. Of itself, visualising does not achieve anything.

However, your brain will tell you that, by making clear what it is that you want to achieve in the long term, you are somehow working towards it. This is a dangerous trap. Take your cousin Mary, who has pronounced each year for many in a row now that her "new year's resolution" is to lose weight.

Everyone (at least for the first few years) gave her a pat on the back and wished her well with that. But then... nothing. She didn't achieve it, and in fact (so I am told) did very little towards actually getting that aspiration off the ground.

The problem, you see, is that by announcing it to the world, talking about it over and over again, and perhaps even by planning to some extent, Mary's brain convinced her that she was actually achieving something.

In fact a study I read recently suggested that you get very nearly the same sense of fulfilment from telling everyone about your plans as you do actually accomplishing them. As a result, your drive to get your goals completed wanes, and you end up back where you started.

If, however, you are aware of this then you can control it. For that reason while, for the moment, we will be looking at the end game - do not think that the process is going to end there for you. We will be going into much more detail to help you achieve what you articulate.

So let us not confuse what I talk about in this letter with goal setting. It is not the same, despite the benefits it can have. Consider this exercise one in aspirations, not in goal setting.

I look forward to receiving your report about where you propose to end up.

All the best,

Uncle Andrew

GETTING ENOUGH DONE IN THE DAY

Dear Thomas,

It is a good question you ask, regarding getting things done during the day, and I appreciate this opportunity to set you on a good path towards productivity.

If you are going to be productive, you need to know what you are trying to produce.

Lots of people trying to be productive seem to miss out on this fairly important step. As a result, they end up being those individuals who want to look very busy but accomplish very little.

Although there may be times where you are forced to embark on such a course (and I have written to you about that before) you are far better served by being productive in valuable areas, rather than just any old thing.

Despite your confidence, you are a junior lawyer. That will change, but for the time being, your methods of productivity are likely to have a number of characteristics.

The first is that you will be productive doing what you are told. Unlike your senior lawyers, you have very little autonomy and so your job is not so much thinking too hard about what you **should** do next, as much as it is thinking about what you **have to** do next.

Provided you have been making the right friends inside your firm, the chances are that you are going to have a constant flow of small(ish) tasks that you are to turn your attention to in order to be a valuable contributor to your firm.

Of course, there are some tasks that you should avoid like the plague. Irrespective of how efficiently you can do these particular things, your efforts are being wasted.

The first in that wasted category are tasks that you should simply not be doing. Filing documents is a classic example - you have an assistant for that, and she (I assume) is the one that should be doing it. Organising events, doing dishes, getting coffees and the like (at the office at least) are similarly unhelpful. Stick to what you are paid to do.

The next things to eliminate are what I'm going to call the "time wasters".

Do you read the paper each morning? Why? Now reading the paper is not inherently bad, but my question is really this - what is in it for you? Similarly positioned are watching the news or "surfing" the internet - what is the benefit? Do those things offer you something tangible and helpful for your professional or personal life? I'm not going to even bother mentioning "social media" in this list, because I think the answer there is obvious.

You might say to me "yes, Uncle Andrew, those things are valuable and here is why", in which case keep doing it (after all - I don't know exactly what you do with these things). But there are many things that most people do, on most days, which are simply a waste of time. The more of those you can eliminate (at best) or minimise (at least) then the more time you will have to devote to things which are really beneficial. That in turn will make you feel more productive through the day because you will simply get more done.

I can quite simply put it this way: everything you say "yes" to, results in something else you need to say "no" to, and vice versa.

There is a limit, of course, to what can be done in terms of eliminating things from your day, and also (much as I hate to admit it) there is a limit to the number of hours you can reasonably expect to be productive in a day.

So at that point you need to consider your efficiency. Are you doing things the right way, or the stupid way?

Here is an example of the right way: you get instructions by telephone to write a letter. You dictate the letter, after which (while it is being typed) you occupy yourself with something useful. You finalise the letter, sign it and give it to your partner to settle and then be sent. The process was efficient, productive, and resulted in the necessary thing being done.

The alternative is the stupid way. It looks something like this: You get an email from a client which you read and then put to one side. Later that day you read it again, refresh your memory, and start to think that you will need to write the letter that has been requested. You ask your secretary to bring you the file, which you put to one side because you are not ready to look at it.

The next morning you remember that you need to write that letter, so you open the email again and re-read it because you have forgotten the specifics. You then dictate the letter, which is returned to you typed. You put the typed letter to one side because you are doing something else, and then edit it later that day after your secretary has gone.

As a result the final changes do not get made until the third day after you received instructions. You get the letter edited and signed after lunch, only to realise that your partner has a "long lunch" that day and will not be able to attend to it the next day. As a result, your secretary needs to update the date on the letter, and the letter is not actually sent until the fourth day after instructions. That assumes your partner has no changes to the letter.

Compare these examples for a moment. In the first, each necessary element of the task is done once. You read the email once, produce a letter and settle it once, and submit it once. It gets signed and sent.

In the next you read the email three times. The letter is amended at least twice, and the time commitment is significantly higher. As well as inefficiency you will also annoy your client who believes (rightly or otherwise) the letter should have been done faster.

Identifying these inefficiencies in your work habits is a critical part of being more productive. The less duplication, double handling, refreshing and the like is done, the better. If you sit down to a task, then do it. Do not get distracted, interrupted or set aside - just get the task done. That is not always possible, but it is certainly possible more often than people think.

These are basic strategies - try putting a few of them into practice. How about in your next report you tell me what wasteful activities you have pruned out of your daily routine? That will give you more time at the office which, in turn, you can start to utilise more profitably.

Regards,

Uncle Andrew

AUTHENTICITY - A MODERN CREATION

Dear Thomas,

Although I appreciate your concerns about my recent strategy for your promotion, I must say I'm a little surprised at your response (and how long it took you to send it).

You mention words like "authentic" and "real" as if my suggestions recently were at odds with your desire to stay yourself. Not so.

I thought that I had made it pretty clear that I was not suggesting you embark on a course of lies, and your inference to the contrary was, frankly, a little rude.

The problem seems to be an issue with your mindset. You seem to think that you are fine "just how you are". While you were thinking this to yourself, I can only assume that little birds landed on your shoulders, music began playing in the background, and your eyes took on a reflective glance long into the distance while you contemplated just how "fine" you were.

Either that, or you have bought into the lie instilled in you by pop culture that you don't have to change in order to succeed. Guess what - it's wrong. I know, you're shocked that television and well meaning friends have not necessarily got it right in that respect.

You need to improve. A lot. In fact, a significant part of your life for the next few years needs to be dedicated to you improving.

No doubt you are thinking that I'm writing now about learning more law, and that I've changed topic? No. What I am trying to do is to convince you that the thinking and strategies which got you to where you find yourself now, are simply insufficient to get you where you need to be next.

As I identified before, one area where you are deficient at the moment is that you lack a genuine interest in sports which are likely to benefit your career. So what I suggest is that, rather than fight me by using some warped sense of "moral high ground" you understand that it is possible to develop a genuine enjoyment and love of these other activities, despite your current attitude towards them.

Your desire to be "authentic" (and despite its recent popularity I've yet to hear a good explanation of what that means) is, to my mind, simply an excuse to tell me that you don't need to improve and take deliberate control of your career.

So rather than simply berate you for accepting a politically correct fiction, I will provide you with some practical tips to embrace your new self.

First, you need to accept that you are not perfect. I appreciate that will be confronting, but let us do our best, okay?

Next I want you to begin learning. Our topic that prompted us here was rugby, and I am sure you can find an abundance of information about rugby everywhere.

You should obviously know the rules, although that's not too important (since you can simply argue with the referee or not, depending on what side you are on).

After that, however, you should learn your local team, its players and its coach. Finally you need to start reading the sports section of the newspaper - this will help you pick up appropriate language for your discussions with your colleagues and boss.

Finally, you need to implement. Start going to games. Cheer for a team. Be happy when they win, and sad when they lose. These emotions will not be hard to genuinely develop, because the chances are high that those around you will have them anyway.

So you see our three step process to a genuine appreciation. Not just rugby, of course, but anything you feel is necessary, but in relation to which you lack a genuine desire.

First you acknowledge the problem. Then you learn about the topic in question. Then you begin participating in the topic.

Those three steps will see you gain an "authentic" love of the game soon enough.

Good luck,

Uncle Andrew

Pro Bono Publico

Dear Thomas,

For a number of months I have been tied up, and so extend my apologies if it has seemed my attention to your career has been waning. I assure you it has not, and I have remained actively interested in some promising remarks that make their way to me each week about your progress.

Among the promising remarks, however, came an interesting observation of some concern to me. Specifically, this individual (who clearly I am not at liberty to name) suggested, with some enthusiasm, that you have volunteered to be an integral part of your firm's "pro bono" program.

I can understand that, in your youth as you are, occasional moments of poor decision making are likely to come up, and in case it has not already dawned upon you, this is one such occasion.

There is, I accept, a current trend towards lawyers and firms engaging in "pro bono" services. But it's not a good plan for anyone interested in their career.

The phrase "pro bono publico" I find to be a fascinating one –"for the public good". I assume you knew that, right?

It is as if the phrase suggests that there is some inherent virtue in providing legal services to a class of clients who are otherwise too uninterested in their lives to earn enough money to pay lawyers the amounts that we ought to be paid.

I do not hate poor people, of course, and I am charitable enough in my own way, but when it comes to the maintenance of the profession it is important that you, nephew, are seen to be dealing with only the highest calibre businesses, government and individuals.

Regrettably for them, those people who may seek to avail themselves of the "pro bono" program have a number of shared characteristics.

First – they have no money, or at least not enough that their desired outcome is possible. This in itself should be seen as an indication that the heavens have declared this individual to be in their position, and it is neither for you nor I to interfere with such a determination.

Second, however, you will find that the nature of the matters which come out of the woodwork in such instances are fencing disputes, petty crime, personal injuries, and what I could only charitably describe as "miscellaneous". That last is, of course, a reference to those aggrieved persons who have a colossal expectation of their own righteous justification, but ultimately have no grievance that is known to a Court of Law.

The final concern about such people is that they generally

require you to completely disregard the advice I have given you recently in connection with your mode of communication. Should you speak in anything above primary school language to them, they will immediately glaze over and, despite any nodding that may ensue, you can be assured they have failed to understand even the most rudimentary parts of your communication.

The result is that any files you might secure in this area are fraught with risk, are of negligible importance, and take you away from matters of greater consequence.

That last is, perhaps, the primary reason that your decision making here came as a shock (I had to sit down, you know) when I learnt of it.

I had thought that I made it clear that your ongoing concern should be to bill as much as possible. You cannot do this with participation in this kind of idealistic program. Although I am sure your firm encourages your participation (it looks good for the firm, after all) I cannot share their view, at least so far as you and your future are concerned.

No doubt there is some kind of public gratitude for the firm's dedication to pro bono work. That is fine, because as a member of the firm you will receive those accolades also, irrespective of whether you personally participate. You just need use phrases like "yes our firm does a lot of pro bono" or "we just got a great win for a client in a pro bono matter". It is here that a strategic use of "we" and "our" can be of significant benefit.

I trust I have explained myself enough here.

When are you going to get promoted?

Regards,

Andrew

A Bit more Diligence Please

Dear nephew,

You have not written to me in some months, but for a singular paragraph telling me that you were "thinking about your options".

I was not sure what you meant by such an assertion, and so I took it upon myself to find out what you have been doing recently. I reached out to a number of people and so now have a reasonable idea of what you were getting at.

Firstly, it appears that you have a new lady friend in your life. Let me say that I am not against you having relationships, however I do need to caution you in that respect.

Who is this person and where did you meet her? I cannot recognise her last name which is, itself, a concerning factor since I am personally familiar with families in your area from whom I would hope that any lasting relationship might come.

Perhaps this is intended to be a short term dalliance on your part? If that is the case, then I will neither congratulate you nor encourage you – you have little time for such flights of fancy and it is beneficial neither for you nor for the lady in question. From your heritage I hope that is not the case, for the expectations in that respect will have been made clear to you for some time. I won't go further on this topic, however, as there are matters of greater concern.

Your senior partners inform me that you have not been attending work over the last couple of weeks due to illness? I am surprised to hear that you have an illness of such apparent seriousness that would lead you to take such a considerable amount of time off work. If you do, I am certainly sympathetic to your situation and wish you well.

However (and if I am wrong in this please forgive me) my other sources lead me to believe that your illness has apparently not prevented you from frequenting various venues with your lady friend, in particular apparently a number of charitable enterprises which she seems to have a history with. You will appreciate that I am, therefore, sceptical of your veracity in that respect.

What is your intention here? I have set out at length for you my thoughts on charitable enterprises in the form of pro bono work, and I assumed that your intelligence would allow you to surmise that similar sentiments would be held with charitable work of a non-legal nature.

In case I overestimated you there, let me be clear: devoting your time to non-profit is a waste. You were built to be a lawyer, and educated and trained accordingly. It is fine for other people to devote their talents to charity, but I object to you doing so when the detriment to your career will be so considerable.

I must insist that, absent you having a serious illness (which in the course of writing the last paragraph I have become even less convinced of) that you return to work immediately. You will, of course, have some ground to make up with your billable hours and you should expect to hear that your leave has had no impact whatsoever on your monthly billings.

On illness generally, however, it seems clear that you think that "sick leave" is there to be taken. It is not. The fact that you may feel unwell on a particular day is irrelevant.

The only excuse for you not to attend the office is if, having been confronted with the direction to stand, your legs actually fail you and you find yourself unable to walk to your office. Only then will I accept any decision not to attend work.

If anybody asks? You just have a mild cold and are fine to continue working. Take whatever pills you need, down whatever cocktail of medication is required to keep you going, but you must be in the office no matter what.

This will distinguish you from your less devoted colleagues and allow you to demonstrate again your commitment to the firm's bottom line.

Do you have any comprehension how much money your "sick leave" is costing the partners of your firm?

No, whatever ill-conceived plan you have had to avoid your duties, you must return to work immediately.

Regards,

Uncle Andrew

STRESS

Dear Thomas,

I am getting the impression from the terse nature of your reports recently that you might be under some stress.

I can understand that might be possible, given the nature of our profession, but it is not really acceptable for you to remain in that state for more than a brief period of time.

So I thought I would write to you to set out some thoughts on how you can manage your stress levels and ensure that you are remaining productive and valuable to your firm.

In my experience, stress stems from a couple of primary causes. First, a mismatch between expectation and reality. Second, a lack of control (which is separate from, but connected to, the first).

There is an important absence from those items, which you may have noticed? Hard work. Hard work is not, of itself, stressful. In fact hard work can be rewarding, beneficial and exciting.

Where hard work seems like it can be stressful is when the mismatch principle comes into play. You see, hard work is only stressful if you are working hard when you didn't think you should be, or you weren't expecting to.

It's stressful when you have to stay late on a night that you were expecting to leave early on. It's stressful when you thought your day would be easy and in fact it becomes full of demands and urgency.

See the difference? If you wake up in the morning with the right anticipation then you will dramatically reduce your stress.

The simple resolution to this problem should be self-evident - arrive at work with an expectation of higher workload and increased demands. In that way, your expectations will be higher than the reality, and if you end up with a day involving slightly less drama or work, then you will feel like it was a good day.

In a sense this is the same process as when you go to see a Hollywood movie that has had plenty of hype. The hype almost never matches the value of the movie itself, and so the best way to ensure you don't feel you are wasting you money is to assume the movie will be terrible. If, on viewing, the movie is passable then you will find yourself with a sense of gladness - the movie was better than expected, and so your decision to see it is vindicated.

Stress can be managed in the same way. Manage your expectations properly and you will be able to manage your stress.

The second issue, especially for young lawyers like you, seems to be connected with control. In one sense this is connected to expectations, but is a particular subset of expectations and worthy of isolated mention.

As I observe young people (yes - that is you) who have been raised in recent decades, a common theme occurs. Each seeks a greater degree of independence and autonomy. Our school systems, of course, are largely designed (having been formulated in the industrial era) to eradicate the kind of independent thinking that many young people are displaying, but nonetheless a lot of early career lawyers seem determined to hold on to the idea that they will have some form of control over what they do in the day and how they do it.

I regret to tell you that the idea of autonomy for someone as inexperienced as you, is complete fiction.

This is where expectations come into play again. You see, the stress and frustration you feel during your day to day life is exacerbated by a constant tension between your desire to do things in a particular way, and the desire of your supervisors to do things in a different way.

As time goes on you will expect to exercise a greater amount of power in decision making and autonomy in your practice. But that time is not yet.

You need to, again, manage your expectations when it comes to these kinds of matters, and understand that as it stands your job is simply to do what you are told, in the way that you are told.

I appreciate that is not necessarily the most fulfilling concept to grapple with, but a proper appreciation of the realities here will absolutely minimise your stress levels so far as they relate to these issues.

Of course these may not be issues. In a sense I am guessing at the sources of your current tension because I know how what many young lawyers go through in their early years while their sense of independence with which they arrived is still causing them issues.

Let me know if this has been helpful.

Is it something else? Perhaps if you were inclined to a little more clarity in your reports to me, I might be able to offer something more specific to assist you.

Best,

Uncle Andrew

Your Apparent Generosity

Dear Thomas,

I received recently a glowing report (not formal you understand, but simply an update that they thought would interest me) from one of your senior lawyers.

It's wonderful, I am told, how prepared you are to give your time and assistance to your colleagues, senior and junior alike, to enable them to complete their various tasks in an efficient and cost effective manner.

In all honesty, I confess to being a little perturbed.

After all this time, it seems that some of my lessons have started to slip your mind, and so I wanted to take this opportunity to refresh your memory before you get too far down the path it appears you have begun.

I can readily see how the qualities referred to are ones which will endear you to your colleagues. However I am forced to ask this question: what are you getting in return?

Generosity for its own sake has no place in the building of a legal career.

Instead, the age old principle (sometimes cast in a negative light) of "you scratch my back and I'll scratch yours" is the appropriate approach to take.

In giving freely of your time and expecting nothing in return, you are simply begging to be taken advantage of.

Why should these leeches get the benefit of your talent (and my guidance, through you, I might add) and offer nothing to you in return?

I can assure you that they will be using your assistance to their own advantage.

Do you believe that when handing in a superior task to their own supervisors they will say "oh Thomas did all the work you should thank him"? Of course not. They will be looking after their own interests, just as you should.

There are two alternative ways to remedy the situation in short order.

The first is to simply stop offering your valuable time up to anyone else (except your employers, of course, in the manner I have described previously).

This has the benefit of being an immediate fix to the problem, and will put you back on track in terms of your own productivity.

Of course, this may take some people aback if it conflicts with your current habits, and so in adopting this process you may find yourself the target of some negative comment. Ordinarily I would not care, but given the glowing reports about you (founded in ignorance, of course, but glowing nonetheless) in this respect I would not recommend this course of action.

The second option for you is to take a more considered and subtle approach to the situation. It is a multi-stage process.

Initially you must start to decrease the amount of time you offer to others. You can do this without being directly rude, of course. Perhaps closing your door more frequently? Or politely mentioning to some enquiries that you are busy at the moment and will come back to them as soon as you can (in case it wasn't obvious, "as soon as you can" is a deliberately non-specific phrase that will allow you an indefinite period of time).

This initial step will allow you to gradually diminish the enquiries without putting people off at a personal level.

The next step is to start to capitalise on the investment you have already made in those people. This simply requires you to seek compensation for your earlier assistance.

You might, for example, begin a discussion by enquiring how that matter you assisted with ended up. You can then follow up with a request for assistance of your own, and use that to your advantage. The subtle reminder of your own contribution to them should be sufficient for all but the most dense of your colleagues to serve as a reminder that they owe you.

This process should allow to begin recapturing your own time, reducing the donation of your time to the careers of others, and ultimately scoring some points through using the compensation you are owed by those you assisted previously.

In all, it's quite a good plan if I might say.

I hope this assists.

Kindest regards,

Uncle Andrew

CONGRATULATIONS ARE IN ORDER

My dear Thomas,

I am most heartened to have received word of your promotion – congratulations. I gather that, in comparison to your peers, this is quite a distinction, as many of them have yet to reach this particular goal despite their efforts.

Without looking to diminish your own achievement, I am glad that my assistance to date has provided for you some practical advantage, and hopefully also a financial one to accompany your new title?

There is a curiosity in legal practice that I am sure has started to dawn upon you, when it comes to promotions, which is this: despite the change in title, there are many who will continue to view you as your junior self. This might include senior secretaries, your peers of a similar age and admission date, and the partners in the firm.

It can be challenging to begin to disrupt this view of you, but here I hope to set out some ways in which you can bring about a shift in attitude.

First I must issue a warning to avoid any kind of arrogance in your new title. Despite my pride in you for achieving it, you should not consider yourself too highly, or those who are capable of doing so may seek to bring you "down a peg or two" to avoid you becoming too enamoured with your own achievements. Rest assured you are still a very junior lawyer, but admittedly a well regarded one.

The first thing you must do is to find a trusted partner in the firm with whom you can discuss the expectations of your new role. Now, do not go into such a conversation with your eyes shut, because it is an opportunity on a number of levels. If you need suggestions for who you should have this conversation with I am happy to make them, but I trust you are up to the task.

Before that happens, however, you need to identify to yourself what you think the new role will entail. Does it empower you to delegate to junior lawyers? Does it give you a marketing budget? Would you like to have the privilege (or burden) of signing mail? These things you must be clear about in your own head before your upcoming conversation, so that you can steer it in the right direction.

The easiest way to determine this is to look at other practitioners who share your new title (ignore their seniority) and see what additional privileges they have. That way you can see what you might be able to see what could be involved in the new role, and pick for yourself those elements which you would prefer to have, and which you would prefer to avoid.

Once those desired aspects of your role are clear in your own mind, it is time to have your discussion. The point of the discussion is to express, in the form of assumptions, the things that you ought to have now. The partner will immediately be able to identify the injustice should others have, for example, a law clerk, and you not. As such you should be able to argue successfully for the parts of the role which you seek to adopt. You will need to use your judgement here gained from knowledge of the partner in question and his idiosyncrasies.

What is the point of all this? Clearly it is to advance yourself within your new role. You see, if you do not take proactive action to solidify your new position, you will find yourself stuck in a role where you perform the same tasks as you always have, and merely have a different title. That, of course, will earn you no respect and even less in terms of career advancement. The title, of itself, is meaningless unless it is accompanied by tangible changes in your position and the nature of your work.

This conversation will also serve as an opportunity to be a visible career-related discussion. That is – when other staff see you talking with this senior partner (you are going to choose a senior partner, I assume) about matters related not to file work but to your career, they will start to make certain assumptions about the path you are on. That is only going to be of benefit to you. Of course, many of those assumptions will be wrong, but in the world of legal practice if people perceive you are on a "fast track" to partnership then they will begin to pay you more respect. After all, if you are made a partner they don't want to burn their relationship with you in advance, do they?

The next thing you must do is ensure that your secretary, now that you have one, is on board with you. Secretaries control much of the information flow around the firm, and so you need to ensure that yours is completely in your corner. If not, you need a new one (I'm sure you can arrange that if required).

Why is this flow of information important? Well, the substance of your performance is less relevant to people around the firm than what people THINK your performance is like. That is where your secretary comes in. She can tell her friends and other secretaries about the really important work you are doing, the high ranking people you are talking to, and the large and complex matters that you are involved in. She should be encouraged to make sure that everyone in the firm is aware of the high calibre work you do, the accolades you receive, and the many happy clients from large corporations that you have.

Naturally this information will get back to the other professional staff, because secretaries are not exactly known for their discretion (which, in this instance, works in your favour). Those other professional staff will, of course, start to have the perception that you ONLY work on those matters of such gravity and that you must be important to the partners and to the firm generally. It is a matter of heuristics (are you familiar with this term?) – if people associate your name with large, complex jobs, many successes and happy, wealthy well-paying clients then you will take on a particular status around the firm which commands respect.

I trust you will start to implement this strategy soon. The benefits are both obvious and tangible.

Regards,

Uncle Andrew

PART FOUR
It's Time to Stop Stuffing Around

THE NEXT PHASE

Dear Thomas,

With your excellent news having arrived, it is now time for us to journey into the next phase of your instruction.

Specifically, we need to start working more diligently on the development of your network and contacts. We'll also start to invest a bit in your habits so far as marketing are concerned. You can expect that, as of now, I will begin to write to you with a greater degree of sophistication than I have in the past, you having demonstrated yourself generally sufficient to the task of legal practice (at least so far as your present employers are concerned).

With your promotion comes a certain added expectation. This need not place any additional burden on you, but rather should be an encouragement to you. With your new title you will be expected to participate in a greater range of extra curricular activities, and more of your own making then simply going where you are told, and doing what is expected.

So I suggest that we take some time to craft, collaboratively, a system for you where your networking activities can thrive, your influence within the firm can increase, and your general habits as a lawyer will continue to improve as they have been to date.

Marketing, of course, is not the only topic that you can expect to learn in this phase of your career. However, it is a significant one and therefore you might anticipate that the topic will take up a considerable amount of our future correspondence.

A word of warning, however. There are a number of flawed approaches to networking and marketing which have begun to prevail in recent times, and I will be correcting you about a few. We will deal with each in more detail over time, but rest assured the plan I propose for you will offer you the greatest benefit, the best contacts, the biggest network, and the most enjoyment.

Yes - I said enjoyment.

You might have started to wonder, I expect, whether any kind of enjoyment was actually relevant to your legal career. I admit that I concealed from you any real impression that I got a sense of happiness from my own career, but I did so to ensure that the work ethic which you came to the office with was one to be admired, respected, and repeated.

That said, it is FROM that call to hard work and diligent practice that I derive my enjoyment, and so those things need not be mutually exclusive - rather, the one is the product of the other.

But I digress.

As I mentioned, modern society would have you tricked into believing that marketing was a function of the tools that you use.

Internet nonsense is playing a prevalent role in the marketing strategies of many lawyers, and much to their detriment. The concept of marketing through social media is as lucrative for a lawyer as entering the lotto repeatedly and taking hours to do it each time.

No, the time wasted by so many young lawyers now in so called "marketing" activities on the internet should be viewed with a lot of scepticism by you and, indeed, by anybody with a jot of common sense.

Principally, the reason is that such activities do not have a chance of developing the necessary depth of relationship to allow you to ask for work from any given individual. Rather, you will sink hundreds of hours into gathering "fans" on your website or whatever, only to find that they have no interest in obtaining legal services from you, and just visited for the fun of it.

In having this view, I obviously will be accused of being archaic in my approach to marketing, but I firmly hold to the belief that the ways that lawyers have successfully marketed their practice for many years is now, and will continue to be, the best and most successful way of gathering a personal practice for you.

The one exception that I will allow is the use of email (except, of course, in our correspondence which should remain an exercise in a more fulsome literary style). Email seems to have become so prevalent now that I cannot escape the reality that it is acceptable to many people, and in my lighter moments even I can begin to accept that it has some usefulness within legal practice.

What you will find as I write to you further is that the strategies I recommend are not those which are modern, or popular, or even time conscious. What they are, however, is tested and proven. They are the strategies that I built my practice on. They are the strategies that your parents used, and generations before us all used to meet people, inspire confidence, develop relationships, and get work through the door. In short - they are the strategies that work.

At this point I would like to offer an important distinction - strategy is a different concept to tactic, which is a different concept to a tool.

Let me illustrate - your strategy might be to develop contacts, your tactic might be to have a lot of coffee, and your tool might be to telephone people asking if they wanted to meet.

There we see that the internet in its various forms falls squarely within the realm of "tool". It might achieve a purpose, but there are better ways to do the same thing, and so I again repeat my most strongly worded suggestion that you avoid the use of internet and social media as a marketing technique.

Enough of what to avoid. The question is what to do?

What I will be writing to you about shortly will be a plan. It is a plan designed to increase your practice. You will need to make more contacts (and the right ones at that), extend those relationships, establish your expertise, and then get the work.

This straightforward summary cannot at all articulate just how difficult this is. But done right, you can have an extremely profitable and well regarded practice in a relatively short space of time.

I look forward to taking you through my thoughts on these and a number of other topics over the coming months.

I trust that you will continue to report to me your efforts, successes and failures as they arise - I look forward to hearing about them and offering my insight where I can.

Kind Regards,

Uncle Andrew

Your so-called "marketing"

Dear Thomas,

One of the things you were learn over time (and in which I will assist you) is to devote your efforts to areas in which they will be most beneficial.

Your firm is, it seems, one of the "new" style firms who believe that an appropriate use of resources is to create a huge quantity of articles and newsletters for consumption by various groups of clients.

I expect that you will be required on occasion to participate in this process. I encourage you, with all possible enthusiasm, to avoid getting sucked into this so called "marketing" program.

There are a number of reasons for this, which I will explain to you.

First – nobody reads those articles. The sheer amount of effort that goes into them would suggest that they are somehow worth the cost of their production. It is untrue. The fact is that the vast majority of such publications are deleted or thrown in the bin straight away. Bear in mind the reality that each person receiving your firm's newsletter also receives about 20 others. Are your firm's articles really that good? I doubt it.

There is a suggestion that it's worth the effort to "get the brand" out there. That assertion is easily defeated by the self-evident truth - people don't hire brands, they hire lawyers.

The next problem is that, even if people did read the articles, they do not achieve anything. Articles don't develop a relationship with clients. Articles don't make clients laugh (normally) and they don't make clients' lives better.

At best, articles from lawyers stuff clients full of yet more legal jargon, with the intention of demonstrating how wonderfully smart the lawyer who wrote it is, in the hope that the demonstrated expertise will prompt the client to say "ah huh – I remember 9 weeks ago I got an article from Joe Bloggs about taxation transactions and so I'm going to send all of my tax work to Joe". Of course this has never happened but, much like entering the lottery, the legal profession continues to waste time with this vain hope.

Now as you will know, I'm not against clients knowing how smart you are - but it has to be in a useful way where you can demonstrate both personality and expertise. Articles generally don't achieve that.

You see, the process of writing articles is a method of self-deception. It has been created by lawyers who know full well that they should be "marketing" but don't have either the knowledge or the courage to do it properly – by developing real relationships with actual people.

So, instead, these same lawyers convince themselves that they are "marketing" by putting pen to paper (or having you do it for them) and then sending out as many copies as they can to as many people as they can think of. In doing so they pat themselves on the back having done some "marketing" and then promptly go back to legal work, having achieved very little.

The final problem for you in particular, Thomas, is that any article you write is unlikely to bear your name. Instead your hard work will bear the name of your supervisor. So even if everything I have said above is incorrect, the production of articles at the behest of others will do your career no good at all.

I will write to you about how marketing endeavours should look, but for the moment I impress upon you – do not get trapped in to a process of article production for your firm, in particular for other people who will take the credit for your efforts, and spend their own time billing their clients heavily.

Best regards,

Uncle Andrew

A Lesson in Networking Functions

My Nephew Thomas,

In your new role I take it that you will have steadily increasing expectations placed on you about your attendance at various functions, conferences, dinners and the like. Naturally you will make yourself available to attend everything you are invited to (with some exceptions which I will come to) because doing otherwise would be foolhardy.

In your tender years however I expect that you will not have had a considerable opportunity to attend such functions and so I thought it proper to give you some gentle instruction as to the goals you should have, the way in which you should conduct yourself and the benefits of each.

Before we come to that however, I should warn you that not all invitations should be accepted by you. There are some in your firm who have limited power and influence of their own, and so will seek to utilise your superior talent at relationship development for themselves. Normally such things are disguised behind "firm" events or the like, but the reality is that you will find yourself being used by lesser partners for their own advantage. As a consequence you will end up devoting significant time and effort towards the advancement of others, when that time and effort should be more properly devoted to your own progress.

I am sure that, by now, you have identified without my assistance those partners who have limited futures within the firm, limited client contacts, and limited ability to expand beyond their current level of income. These are not, of course, the kind of partners to whom you need be attached. Ultimately you will surpass them, provided they are not propped up by you to your own disadvantage during this time. And so, while I advise to accept many invitations to functions, do not accept them all.

Of course you cannot simply disregard a direct request from your superiors, however you can make it your business to be unavailable for such events as frequently as possible without casting suspicion on your motives.

Those more advanced and better performing partners, of course, will understand more appropriately and personally that your intention at any networking function is to expand your own personal contacts to your own advantage. As a result, although they will be accommodating to that goal they are unlikely to permit you to intrude on their own contacts and so you need not be concerned about stepping on anyone's toes in terms of your personal endeavours. These partners can provide you with a lot of useful information in preparation for any event that you are likely to attend.

My first advice for you then is to ensure that you extract whatever information you can about the likely people you will get to meet at any function, and then use your own resources (which these days I expect will include the "internet") to provide yourself with a necessary and helpful foundation to topics of conversation with those people.

It would be foolish in the extreme to select for yourself the oldest and most senior people at any given function as your targets for conversation. There are a number of reasons for this.

First, they are unlikely to respond to you favourably. You may be charming and young and enthusiastic, but these men (and occasionally women) have been through more functions than days you have been alive. You are, quite simply, not interesting to them. You can offer them nothing. Therefore, do not waste your time in idle pleasantries with people whose time you are wasting.

The second reason is that the majority of these superior networking targets will be well acquainted with a number of their peers and will likely be extremely difficult to approach – most likely so difficult that in approaching them at all you will need to intrude on an existing conversation which will probably be considered rude. That is hardly an auspicious beginning.

No, rather seek to select for yourself some individuals older than you, but not too much older, who are in the position of middle to upper management but not yet advanced to the highest levels of seniority. These are your targets. You might like to select 3 or 4, and possibly up to 5 or 6 that you will conduct your research on. You should expect that some of those you identify will not attend, and others will be unavailable to you.

The purpose of the research is, of course, to allow you to make conversation that is of interest to the target, at least at first. Of course the end goal for any such discussion is to ensure that throughout the course of the conversation you mention your relationship to me, your recent Court appearances, and the most complex matters that you have had any contact with whatsoever.

Judicious use of the words "we" and "our" here will, as I have mentioned before, do you in good stead. Of course from time to time you need to allow your counterpart to speak of matters relating to themselves, but principally I have learnt that little is more interesting to others than a lawyer who has a good number of stories to tell about their recent engagements.

It takes practice, of course, to steer conversations in that way towards your desired discussion points, but it is certainly possible. If you need to practice this then politicians are masters at the art of ensuring that any question on any topic gets an answer which is "on message". So it should be with you – your "message" is to communicate your prowess as a lawyer.

Now, you have considered what to say and who to say it to – but what do you actually do when you get to the function?

I take it you consider yourself to be quite practised at "holding your drink" from your efforts at college? Well, I can tell you without a shadow of a doubt that you have as much experience with drinking as a gnat has with the fine arts.

Lawyers, and often their clients, are renowned for their ability to consume drink without significant impairment, and you will need to learn this art if you are going to be able to excel at networking events.

When you arrive at any function you must immediately get a drink. Get used to eating, talking, and shaking hands while holding a drink, because you are going to do a lot of it. If you happen to see your target individuals first, then get the same drink as them. If not, it doesn't matter that much.

It has become popular for some lawyers to consider themselves too good to share a drink with their colleagues. Personally I find it offensive. Lawyers have a long and glorious history of consuming fine alcoholic beverages and the people that are against it for some reason have clearly had severely deficient training in that area.

The consumption of drink is not, of course, for the purpose of getting drunk. Indeed, you should ensure that you do not get drunk at a function, despite the amount of drink you consume. The consumption of drink is to ensure that you are appropriately relaxed and gregarious. The first a result of the chemicals you imbibe, and the second a consequence of the social construct which permits strangers who otherwise have little in common to develop relationships around the common undertaking of drinking.

A glass of soda does not create the same atmosphere, and whatever myth about "staying sharp" might have been told to you, it is no doubt from the weak willed who find themselves unable to sensibly consume liquor without adverse consequence.

This letter has now been far too long, and my hand is tiring. I expect my point is well made, and you will take it from there.

Best Regards,

Uncle Andrew

Making it Rain

My dear Thomas,

I hear you have excelled yourself at recent functions with your firm, and so perhaps I need not devote too much time in this letter towards your continued education in that respect.

Lest you think, however, that you may now rest on your laurels, can I commend you not to relax your efforts at networking functions. However few events you have now attended with success, there are infinitely more coming to you for the remainder of your career, and so I would encourage you to be mindful of your presence at functions.

On a broader topic that may now interest you, however, I thought it was time to devote a little attention towards business development in the broader sense.

There are many levers that lawyers tug at in the modern legal market to try and coax, cajole and trick people into walking through their doors to engage their legal services.

The first lever is an effort to be cost competitive. Stay away from it. I have spoken before to you about things like conveyancing where this practice of "cheapest is best" is rife, and so I again exhort you not to be tempted towards the gutter end of legal practice. I know many fine successful property lawyers, and none of them are competitive in that way.

Should you choose to become the Walmart of legal services, providing what is effectively the cheapest possible service to the largest number of people you can find, then you should be prepared for my ongoing assistance to end.

Not only will I be ignorant of what you are seeking to achieve and therefore unable to provide any insight, I will also have to form the opinion that your overarching goal is to bring our noble profession into disrepute.

The next thing that I have noticed recently (with the rise and rise of the internet) is that there is a heavy focus on internet marketing. This might include using such tools as "social media" to engage in some form of widespread marketing. Again I have yet to hear of any success in this area. The number of "twitter" followers somebody has seems to me to bear little resemblance to their talent as an attorney and far more correlation to the size of their ego.

Someone recently invited me at an event to join them on "LinkedIn" – when I expressed my ignorance of that tool, they actually seemed surprised. I, in turn, expressed surprise that they continually wasted precious billable hours on what appears to me to be a glorified newspaper where nobody with any talent gets to contribute. Ultimately we agreed to disagree on that one.

For over 30 years I have used a simple strategy that I'm going to share with you.

First – be seen as the best. Naturally this doesn't mean you have to BE the best, but if people THINK you are then that's fine for these purposes. Hopefully your skill will catch up with your presentation soon enough, but for now you will need to have a certain amount of bluff. Clearly I am not advocating deception here, but you need to ensure that nobody leaves a conversation without absolute certainty that you are the best in your field.

There are some modest types who think this looks bad – ignore them. They are the retiring flowers who will ultimately fade into insignificance. They might be technicians in their fields, but if they won't tell anybody that then they are going to fail.

Next – while you are being seen as the best, ensure that your competition is seen as less desirable in some way. I'm sure you are smart enough to know that defaming your competition is an unsafe strategy. However you can achieve the same result with a clever use of innuendo.

For example "oh yeah I know Mr Smith, he's that lawyer over at Smith and Barnes, isn't he? – I was just reading an interesting case where I think they acted for the guy got a penalty of $1m ordered against him".

See how it works? You associate the firm with a bad result,

thus casting doubt on their talent even though what you have said is completely innocuous and truthful.

Obviously you will lose as many cases as anybody else, but clients are ignorant of that kind of thing. Having planted the seed about your competitors in that way, it's not hard to grow.

Finally, my strategy involved getting to know the right people. For you these will be men who are a few years older and have a bit more money to spend. Your job is to locate yourself among them. Join clubs, associations and whatever else you can find (you may need to play a sport Thomas, and you'll just have to get over that).

There you have it. You know what to say and who to say it to.

Simply repeat the process at every available opportunity, and you will soon find yourself well regarded wherever you go.

I look forward to hearing about your progress in your next letter, which I would like to remind you to send since you still seem to forget the regularity of communication that is required to ensure that our relationship is beneficial to you.

Regards,

Uncle Andrew

Earning More Money

Thomas,

I hear that you have been whining a bit to various people about your recent pay packet? I am baffled, I admit, that your response to adversity is to complain about it.

How about instead of complaining, you actually do something about it?

Nothing bothers me more than young people who develop a sense of entitlement, Thomas, so I hope that you don't intend to make a habit of this.

Firstly – what is the problem with your salary? I know what it is, and frankly it far exceeds what I was paid at your level. I have compared it to a number of competitors around the place and enquired with others I know (do not be concerned, as I did not tell them who my enquiry was regarding) – it appears to them and to me that you are paid very well.

So I would first counsel you to consider whether your complaint is well founded or whether it is simply the dreaming of a young person who doesn't think they need to work harder to get more in life.

That all said (I am here to help you after all) I wanted to offer you a few strategies to try and justify an increase in salary for you. Rest assured that on this topic I do not intend to get involved directly on your behalf – you are a grown up now and so you need to develop your own resources in this regard.

The first and most obvious thing you could do is threaten to leave. This is a high risk strategy of course, but can be effective. If you have been, as I suggested earlier, developing the necessary relationships within your firm, then this kind of approach should really be unnecessary.

I assume for the moment that you have no desire to leave, and no desire to make such a threat.

And so the next question becomes how to entice more funds from your employers.

As a former employer myself, I imagine that I have a different perspective to you on this issue. The reality is that as an employer I do not want to pay you any greater amount than I have already offered to you.

In fact, I want to pay you as little as I can to ensure that your presence in my firm is as profitable as possible for me. The billable hours you put in would, of course, contribute directly to my own hip pocket.

So what do you need to do in order to make a compelling case for a better salary?

It's simple – make your partners more money.

There's a few ways you can do this. I've written before about, and presume we are now agreed that, time in the office is time well spent.

I'm sure that you are billing as much as possible during that time, because nobody in our family has done otherwise for many years.

I'm also assuming that, as I have advised previously, you have relieved yourself of any requirement to do free or non-billable tasks in the office, to the extent that is possible.

So what are you going to do?

You need to figure out how to either bring more money in the door, or assist the firm to spend less money.

You can achieve the former through leveraging your contacts and bringing new clients in. At your age, each of your parents and I had a number of very large companies for whom we were acting, which worked heavily in our favour when it came to the financial side of negotiations with our (then) respective employers.

You could also make more money for the firm by persuading them to increase your charge-out rate to a higher figure, which in turn would translate to greater earning capacity and an increased salary for you.

In terms of reducing costs, your options involve increasing efficiency and decreasing cost. Ensure that the firm is lean in every department except for your salary.

Finally, have you considered pointing to your peers' salaries and observing how unfair their additional amounts are compared to yours?

The definition of "peers" here probably needs some attention – if you are an associate, then all associates are fair game, irrespective of whether they are significantly more senior than you. Provided your output is similar in terms of billable time, then you are all on the same playing field when it comes to this discussion.

Those are my thoughts on some options for you.

The easiest to implement are likely going to be increasing your charge-out rate, which itself can involve a comparison to peers exercise as I have just described.

Good luck – this is excellent practice at complex negotiation, so I trust you will acquit yourself admirably.

Profitable wishes,

Andrew

Your New Supervisor

Thomas,

I read with pleasure your recent update about getting a bit of exposure to the mergers and acquisitions team.

I recognise that, for many, a stint in the world of residential property conveyancing might contain a small amount of joy, but as I am sure you know the conveyance of property is really not something which warrants the attention of senior lawyers. After all, how hard can it really be? No, I think that many respectable lawyers have had their careers ruined by spending too much time in an industry which, in reality, could have its work done by secretaries and paralegals.

The role of the lawyer in such an environment becomes not one of legal advice and assistance, but normally a counselling or "agony aunt" role where person after person call for updates on the status of their conveyance, having not read anything that you have sent to them and failing to understand the basic principle that "no news is good news".

I am, therefore, very happy with your move to a group where complex and satisfying legal work will be performed. As you know the area is close to my heart, and while I cannot claim any exertion of influence on you to take up the field, I am grateful that you have decided to continue your family's tradition of high-end corporate work. I say this, of course, on the assumption that you will be staying in the group that you have now moved to, rather than taking up an interest in yet another field (and at this point I might caution you that moving fields too frequently is unlikely to be beneficial to your career, because at each step you will become, once again, junior – so stay where you are).

I did have one concern that I wanted to voice with you, however, about the latest move.

I asked a former colleague of mine to give me some information about that group, and it appears to be headed up by one Ms Jessica Robinson.

Now, at this point I would like to impress upon you that these letters are to be kept confidential (at least, by you), for the opinion I am about to express, although widely held, is rarely articulated. I set it out here in the hope that you can learn from it, but would be most unimpressed if I were to find it repeated back to me by a third party.

Ms Robinson, according to my research, fits the essential bill of a modern female solicitor. Of course, when I was admitted, the majority of the profession was male and so the issues I am about to bring up did not generally arise.

Certain types of female lawyer have been a thorn in the side of the profession. Your mother, of course, is an exception.

She bears a singularly intelligent mind and her elevation to the bench was well deserved. I wish I could say the same for the majority of women in the law, but I cannot. So although I am sure that there are exceptions to the things I am about to raise, I shall refer in this letter to "females" or female lawyers in the generic terminology.

Young women who have devoted themselves to legal practice tend to share common characteristics which, while first appearing to resemble those which male practitioners have, are subtly different and ultimately destructive. Despite current politically correct thinking, the reality is that men and women are different. My wife was different from me (or I from her, depending on your point of view), and that worked to our advantage. Of course it took us a few years to get used to the boundaries, roles, strengths and weaknesses between us. But once we did, acknowledging and working within those concepts contributed to our success in many areas.

Unfortunately, young women over the last few decades have now been lied to consistently.

That lie takes the following form:

"Here is a successful person. They appear to have the following characteristics, so far as we can tell from looking at them. You, too, can be successful if you simply adopt those same characteristics".

Can you see the falsehood? Of course, it is a falsehood that applies not just to women, but to men. Where the gender of the recipient becomes relevant is this: the example of the successful person might be male, and the reader might be female.

In law that is more likely because, for whatever reason, most top lawyers are male. The examples of success that are presented are therefore from a male perspective, not from a female perspective.

As a result we look at a man, we identify his characteristics, and young women are told to emulate those in order to succeed.

The lie here exists because the copying of a successful person at the surface level does not therefore make you successful. I could go and give a certain speech called "I have a dream" today, and the effect of it would be very different to what occurred at its original presentation. Likewise you could speak words to a judge, and they would be received differently to that of a senior barrister using the same language.

It's a particularly pervasive lie, because it tugs at the desires of most young lawyers - the desire to be successful in their career, and make it "to the top".

In the desire to copy success, otherwise acceptable characteristics become distorted in translation, and ultimately turn negative. So far, of course, this is not an issue about women lawyers but about everyone who seeks to succeed by replication. That being the case, let me describe some examples so I can explain how this looks in practice.

Many successful lawyers have a high quality output. Their letters are error free, they have sound legal principles, and they advise their clients well. However, the stereotypical female lawyer looks at that, desires that outcome, and turns it into a tendency to micro manage.

Now, male practitioners have between them a certain amount of trust, and even when delegating to junior staff such as yourself it is expected that you will make yourself aware of the necessary laws and procedures, and then produce a document in compliance with them. As a result, delegation occurs smoothly and effectively, the job gets done, and generally speaking it goes just fine. This trust, however, is not immediately apparent when the female lawyer comes to copy the desired outcome (work of high quality).

Females, however, might have no such trust. In fact they could have a tendency to so closely scrutinise every step of the task done that I sometimes wonder why they just don't do it themselves. The result is that the necessity of high quality output becomes not a function of trust and interaction, but a factor that results from an intense micromanaging process. Every word, step, decision and legal principle you adopt needs to be checked, rechecked and approved. So be warned – irrespective of the quality of what you produce you need to be prepared to back up every decision you make.

Here we see how the positive quality of high value legal work can be twisted and turned into a process that, within the team, cannot be sustained and destroys the confidence of the young lawyer.

Which leads to another quality I must raise – bossiness. Somehow, female solicitors seem to have taken positive qualities such as confidence and leadership, and turned them into some kind of mockery which tends to manifest itself as rudeness.

But take the wealthy and successful that we see. I'll give you a modern example: Sir Richard Branson. We see a confident, brash, tough decision maker on the surface. As a result, if we seek to copy him in that respect we might find ourselves doing those things without any nuanced and complex understanding of what lies underneath his skin.

Confidence is a positive trait, but only if you are confident. You cannot feign confidence, any more than you can feign legal knowledge. Ultimately you will be caught out; discovered; unveiled as an imposter. The result is that the lie then becomes far worse than the truth, in that now you not only lack confidence, you lack authenticity as well.

What female practitioners seem to want is to exhibit the qualities that they think male practitioners have. In doing so, of course, they are "faking it" which is not their strong suit. The result is that they become loud, abrasive, and generally difficult to reason with or even have a rational conversation with. Here you see how many female lawyers are their own worst enemies. In their desire for increased status, power and money they utilise methods that simply do not work for them. They fail to see their unique strengths and, as a result, ultimately have to crash and bash their way to seniority, rather than earning it through respect and relationship.

The above is not theoretical. I have seen it now dozens, if not hundreds, of times. By all accounts your new workgroup partner falls into this category, and so I have spent now a deal of time explaining why that could be a problem for you.

In case it was not obvious, however, the reason this becomes a problem for you (rather than just her) is that you will be tarnished by her errors. If you both go to a client lunch, will you not be viewed as a team? If people cannot resonate with her, they will not bother trying to with you. Likewise within the office, although you might be given a greater degree of "benefit of the doubt", your career will ultimately be hampered by her and the way she conducts her practice.

As a result of all this, I warn you to carefully consider your attachment to this partner. Are there other options available to you within the same group? Perhaps you might try to take up as much of the male partner's work as possible, finding yourself then too busy to spend too much time with Ms

Robinson.

There is no guarantee that the male partner will be competent, of course, but at least the odds are higher that he would be authentic. Most likely you will be able to work more closely with him (if he exists) and that will be better in the long run for you.

I caution you again not to express the views in this letter to anyone. Despite their truth, it has become unpopular to hold such opinions and you might get us both some unwanted scrutiny.

Your concerned uncle,

Andrew

ABOUT YOUR EXTRA CURRICULAR ACTIVITIES

Dear Thomas,

I see from your recent update that your recent negotiations were unsuccessful regarding your salary?

Although I am sympathetic, I suggest you get back to work now and not get distracted. Perhaps had you negotiated better at the outset, you might not find yourself in this position.

There will be future opportunities to discuss money, but for now I wanted to briefly address something that has come to my attention regarding your non-work life.

Apparently you have been devoting a good amount of time to playing computer games? Even to the extent that you have recently attended large functions full of other young (and, disturbingly, less young) people who play those games?

I confess I am baffled.

What is it that you seem to think makes this an appropriate course of conduct for a young lawyer seeking to advance?

On one level I could initially see that there would be potential marketing activities available through such pursuits, but when considered further I realised that the demographic of the people attending such functions is almost exclusively made up of people who cannot afford legal services.

So why are you doing this?

I can only fathom that you are trying somehow to cling to some childhood fancy of being a professional "gamer" – a story once told to me by your parents.

If that is the case, I strongly urge you to let go of that desire, right now.

Is it possible that you have an addiction? I have read about such things, and so I do not want to minimise any struggle you are having by assuming only that you are making a conscious choice down this path.

Either way, end this now. Your habits, as I have written before, now need to be centred only on activities that are beneficial to your career, not those which comprise a waste of time by people who will never ever be successful in life.

If indeed this is an addiction of some sort please let me know and the family will arrange the best counselling we can for you. Please desist from this destructive behaviour.

With continuing concern,

Andrew

Vanity Metrics

Dear Thomas,

I wrote to you not long ago about the traps of internet "marketing" and how you should avoid it.

There is a connected, but slightly different, issue I wanted to touch on today. It is the idea of vanity metrics. You see, legal practice can be a place for some very significant egos to play. As a result, the comparison of the biggest matter, the largest payout, the most significant deal - these are issues which come up time and again.

One area you will find yourself trying to compete is in the size of your contact list.

How is the internet relevant to this? Well, despite being mostly ignorant of it, I have observed many people trying to achieve bigger numbers in their "followers" and "likes" and "connections" and similar targets.

I have written previously about my thoughts of various endeavours on the internet, so I shall not repeat myself in great detail.

But there is an insidious issue here - a focus on vanity metrics.

Now in my own firm before my departure I was cautious to

stay away from involvement in issues relating to social media. On the one hand they would simply irritate me. On the other, I was comfortable enough to admit my own ignorance such that my involvement would be a burden on everyone.

However, I did keep my eye on projects revolving around social media, and I had serious concerns with a number of matters put forward.

Principally I was concerned about numbers. Not their increase, but their meaning.

You see, our marketing team would try to convince upper management that in the social media world the increasing number of "likes" and "pins" and "tweets" and other nonsense was a symbol of some kind of success.

However, the reality was quite different.

In reality, our marketing team was purchasing enough advertising space on the internet to sink a battleship, and so an increased awareness of our brand was inevitable and expected.

But what was the real outcome of these endeavours? If I managed to get 1000 people connected with me on "LinkedIn" does that somehow make me a success? Surely not. Success is determined not by the number of our fictitious connections but by the number of our real relationships that generate an income for us or our firm.

So with those ill-informed opinions of mine about social media, the most I can caution you about the topic of my ignorance is this: be wary of the trap of vanity metrics.

Sure, having 2000 followers (is that a lot of followers?) may give one a warm feeling inside, as may a few dozen "likes" on a particular publication - but what good is it?

The power of social media, if any, lies not in the number of followers, likes, shares or anything else - unless those are converted into paying work.

I accept that the day of the powerful law firm brand is over, or at least it is very nearly over.

Firm brand is being replaced by personal relationship (which, ironically, is what there was before the rise of the mega-firm anyway), and I expect you have many tactics at your disposal that I do not in that regard - but I strongly caution you not to swell your head on the basis of meaningless numbers, but on the basis of real outcomes.

It seems to me that the power of social media lies in the ability for the individual to make connections, but the power of the individual remains (as it always has) in the ability to develop those connections to something profitable.

In that sense the overall marketing strategy has not changed, just the tactics have.

Do you use social media? What do you do with it (please tell me it does not involve pictures of your food)?

Best,

Uncle Andrew

BUILDING YOUR NETWORK

Dear Thomas,

Previously I have provided you with some advice about your habits in attending networking functions. Functions are one thing, however as you progress it is time to discuss the possibilities that now open to you above and beyond the mere attendance at events.

Of course building a network, of itself, has limited value. Another time I will write to you about what to do with your network as you expand it, however for now let us simply discuss the simple proposition of networking: the more people you know, and the better you know them, the greater your overall influence and power is.

I hope by now these things are not controversial propositions for you, as even the most lacklustre lawyers accept these basic ideas.

I want to contrast what I have just said with the "vanity metrics" that I have written to you about previously.

In case you did not notice it in my earlier letter on the topic, the first and most obvious place you need to develop relationships with people is in your own firm. Even aside from the fact that professional colleagues are a significant potential source of referral work, having good relationships amongst your colleagues is simply good sense. They are, after all, the evangelists for your reputation - when existing clients ask them who to use in your area, who should they mention? You - or one of your colleagues?

To that end, I recommend you form a list (if only in your head) of who the people are that you see most often distributing work amongst you and your colleagues, and deciding on a strategy to get them involved in your own development.

At first, that is probably going to involve simply being known to them. Attending firm events, having discussions with them, and generally "getting to know them" are all perfectly valid ways to start.

The next thing they need to know, however, is whether sending you work (or requesting of your partner that you be involved) is safe for them and their client. Do not forget that by getting you involved, you are basically responsible for their reputation, just as they are for yours. So you need to ensure that your work excels in every way.

Over time, if you can stay in good stead, deliver good value and do so repeatedly - you will become a mainstay for internal referrals of work within your office.

Then, of course, we need to do likewise with your external network.

By now, you will have developed a list of contacts and people who will take your call, that at least on the surface you have a good and congenial relationship with.

The question is how to turn those congenial relationships into warm leads and then to paying work.

Firstly - it's a long process. As much as bravado and confidence will get you a certain way, the kind of work you do means that a great deal of trust is required to get you involved over the many other choices that are available.

Therefore your job, similar to your internal referrers, is first to exist. You need to be known, and front of mind. The tools you use to do that might vary (yes - I accept the reality that you might use the internet) but the goal, no matter what you use, is to have discussions with people and ensure that you are known to them. That includes them knowing what you do for a living, not just that you exist.

Beyond that you need to find a way of developing trust. That can be hard in this kind of work (and especially if you don't have a good relationship to begin with) but, much like a personal relationship, it cannot be rushed. So take your time, offer some advice, hints, tips, value or things that are otherwise useful (but without exposing yourself to risk) and play on the trigger of what is called "reciprocity". Have you heard of that? It's what happens when your wife says "I love you" and you feel obliged to say "I love you too" even if you weren't going to in the first place. People will feel a subtle obligation to "pay you back" - it's sounds manipulative but isn't really - it's just a natural tendency of people.

Finally, you need to be ready to say what you can offer in terms of legal work. This is where a lot of lawyers fail because, despite our pride and ego when we are alone, it seems to transform into some false sense of humility when confronted with a real opportunity to sell our services.

Try and get over that.

It does not mean you need to become a blowhard that everybody hates, but simply that you need to be ready to step up to the plate if the opportunity arises.

Beyond those strategies, you also need to know when you are getting nowhere with a particular person. After all, as your network grows you simply will not be able to keep up with everyone that you have met, and you need to make sure that your time is being spent where it is most valuable. I expect that will include maintaining relationships with good referrers, and trying as best you can to develop relationships with new ones. That should keep you plenty busy.

Oh yes - do not forget that the partners you are working with internally will have the potential to give you "warm" introductions to potential referrers. It is another reason that having good internal relationships can assist you.

Perhaps in your report next you can tell me which partners in your firm you are planning on focusing on, and I can see what I can find out about them for you?

All the best,

Uncle Andrew

YOUR COURTROOM APPEARANCE

My dear Thomas,

I must say I was surprised to hear that, as part of the mergers and acquisitions team, you were called upon for a Court appearance.

You need not be concerned, however, as I am most heartened to hear of your debut as an advocate for your client. The relatively inconsequential nature of the hearing is irrelevant – the fact is that you have now performed what is, in essence, the primary duty of the legal professional. Drafting documents, advising and otherwise flitting hither and thither at the instructions of clients is all well and good, but nothing gets the blood pumping quite like a Court appearance.

I heard about your efforts fairly quickly, since half the other lawyers in the room are well known to me and you to them. They spoke highly of your brief encounter with the (apparently benevolent) Judge, and say that you acquitted yourself with decorum.

It behoves me, however, to take a few minutes to instruct you in the art of advocacy, to ensure that subsequent appearances of yours are not troubled by unnecessary concerns.

The first consideration you must have is the purpose for your appearance. Now, the naïve and idealistic would have it that the sole purpose of your appearance is to further your client's interests and discharge your duty to the Court in the process. That is, of course, the textbook answer to the question and has little bearing on the realities of legal practice.

Of course your client's interests are part of your job there, and an important one. That is not, however, the only piece of the puzzle.

No, there are a number of opportunities inherent in a Court appearance which, apparently, escape the attention of some.

The first opportunity arises not at the hearing but before it. I take it that, prior to the Court being called, it is still the habit of lawyers to gather and to interact with one another casually? Naturally, this time spent is explained to the client as a necessary precaution of arriving at Court in a timely fashion (which is probably right), but the reality is that the opportunity to interact with other more senior lawyers is a critical one which cannot be missed by any lawyer looking to advance in their career. The eminent lawyers who often gather prior to the hearing are often a source of prestige and information, and by virtue of those things they are also a source of career advancement for you.

Now it would, of course, be completely inappropriate for someone of your tender years in the profession to interact with such senior lawyers without an appropriate introduction.

Fortunately for you, I have already begun the process of making you known, that you need not be concerned with introducing yourself to a number of well-known counsel in your vicinity. I attach to this letter a list of their names, chambers, and a description of their appearances [editor's note – despite my best efforts, the attachment to this letter appears to have gone missing for good and I could not locate it].

If you have the good fortune to make another Court appearance, I am sure that you will utilise this information to your advantage, and prior to your appearance make it your habit to revisit this list and identify one or two possible candidates for a worthwhile discussion about whatever they choose to speak with you about. You can be assured that I will speak highly of you to them, and so your reputation (by which of course I mean the reputation I am building for you) will precede you to a degree.

The next opportunity that you ought not take for granted is the opportunity to make yourself known to the judges. Be warned, however – if you do this in a manner that is repugnant I will instantly distance myself from you. Judges are the decision makers. They are the power brokers, the influencers and the managers of the legal profession. When you were admitted to practice you'll remember that you were sworn in a Courtroom when you took your oath. That should be enough indication to you that the area of your legal practice is irrelevant when it comes to this – developing a beneficial relationship with judges is a critical component of your growth. Judges, of course, are most often available for interaction through Courtrooms and so that is where the opportunity arises.

How do you develop relationship with a judge in a Court? Carefully. Obviously you must acquit your duties properly, or the Judge will consider you to be an inferior lawyer. It is here that you must consider developing your advocacy skills at every opportunity, which I appreciate will be difficult (but not impossible) in your current role. However, what you need to be is impressive without being obsequious. Forceful but simultaneously respectful. The initial goal you must have is to become known to the Judges, but also to have a reputation as an effective and admirable lawyer. Over time you will have more opportunities to capitalise on those initial impressions, which we can talk about later.

I trust you are coming to the family function later this year? We are looking forward to seeing you, and I would like a chance to discuss some things with you in person.

Regards,

Uncle Andrew

ANOTHER PROMOTION... SORT OF

Dear Thomas,

I was confused by your latest report where you proudly announced your promotion.

I confess the title you describe is unknown to me, as I have never had such a title nor promoted any other person to that position.

To satisfy my curiosity, I had to enquire of your parents who informed me that the title you have been given is to recognise a senior person in the firm but not yet one equivalent to that of partner.

If that is correct then I congratulate you.

However, beyond that, my enquiries also suggest that the position is one frequently given to those who have no desire to become partner, or who have been assured by their firms that promotion to partner will never be offered them.

Surely that is not the case with you?

I had thought that your career path would have been fairly obvious, and that taking some kind of strange alternative would not be something that would enter your mind without at least consulting with me?

I appreciate that in modern legal practice there are many alternatives available in terms of careers. However, in our family, such paths are not viable options. The choices made by your parents, myself and innumerable other members of your family are, I am sure, sufficient for you also.

The problem, Thomas, is this: if you are going to be successful in your career, then you need to be a partner.

Partners make more money.

Partners develop more contacts to assist them.

Partners have more power, more influence, and decidedly more ability to improve their lives than any other form of lawyer (I am ignoring here the situation of a barrister who is on a different path entirely).

It is clear that aspiring to partnership is the superior choice, and so I am left with this question: did you make the choice to request this "promotion" or was it foist upon you?

If the former, then I must strongly recommend that you unmake the choice and indicate an alternative preference to your senior partners. This will include admitting you made a mistake, no doubt, but that is not avoidable at this point.

If the latter, however, then we will need to explore more fully what issues arose that were considered to render you unsuitable for partnership, and how we can go about changing that perception.

Please advise so we can take the matter further as required.

Yours faithfully,

Uncle Andrew

PART FIVE
WHAT GOT YOU HERE, WON'T GET YOU THERE

THE HOME STRETCH

Dear Thomas,

Well, you have reached a level of achievement that many would be envious of. I congratulate you. I remain disappointed that you have chosen to take the promotion option that we recently discussed, but I have an appreciation of your reasoning and I understand your motivations.

If you choose not to pursue some of the trappings of legal practice then that is a matter for you. I took a different path, but at this point you are now a grown man, capable of making your own decisions and dealing with the consequences.

By now I think you have mastered the fundamentals of mindset, of emotional resilience, of your working habits, and of developing your network and practice area diligently. Despite your recent decision, I hope that those lessons will remain useful.

So we need to ask the question of ourselves - what shall we engage with for this phase of your career? You already know where I stand, and hopefully where you do as well, on the majority of common issues in practice.

One idea that occurred to me is to begin discussing with you the issues that will arise as you transition from worker to manager.

We have focused heavily in our correspondence to date on issues arising strictly within the confines of legal practice, but from now on you will be dealing not only with clients and legal matters, but also a great deal more with other people within your own firm.

Probably you have already seen a glimpse of this in your practice to date, but I expect you have mostly been protected from it.

I am making an assumption here, but it is fairly commonplace amongst lawyers that promotions are distributed not on the individual's overall capacity as a leader and a manager, but rather by reference to their practice and their billable time.

Rightly or wrongly, that has a tendency to leave many recently promoted lawyers up a particular creek, without a particular instrument.

Your training, experience and knowledge all result in you being an adept and proficient lawyer. They have not, however, prepared you for management.

I recall when I was promoted to partner, I was similarly ill equipped to deal with people. I had a booming practice, significant clients, and a sharp legal mind. But my own deficiencies lead to a number of significant issues when it came to managing my staff, my team, and my responsibilities to the people around me.

With that experience in mind, I thought we might start on a course of learning about people, in particular with a focus on how to get the best from those around you.

As a corollary to that, I think we should also take a little time to consider how you can now be contributing to the overall success of your firm, as your position has now shifted and so has your ability to contribute in different areas.

What do you think?

Best,

Uncle Andrew

GET THE RIGHT PEOPLE AROUND YOU

Dear Thomas,

I'm glad you like my idea, and I appreciate the enthusiasm you showed for it.

The first thing I thought we could consider is the question of who is around you.

There is a phrase going around at the moment (I don't know where it started) that you are the "average of the 5 people closest to you".

I don't know if that is inherently right, but it illustrates an important point: the people around you will affect how you conduct your business and your life.

I should stress that I am not only talking about lawyers here. During your junior years, the chances are that you did not have much flexibility when it came to your personal assistant (although I recall I gave you some advice in that respect)? Hopefully now, in a firm like yours, you will be given an opportunity to select your own rather than just taking whatever (um - whoever) walks through the door.

Similarly, it relates to junior lawyers working in your team.

We will get to delegation soon enough, but the team you surround yourself with is critical to your ongoing success as a lawyer. Unlike your personal assistants, you might have less ability to influence this, but you are certainly not powerless.

So having established the importance of the issue, the question is this: what kind of people should make up your team?

Your personal assistant is critical to your team. She (it's normally a she - don't write to me about political correctness again please) is the one who shields you from clients and colleagues alike, who presents your professional image to the outside world, who types your letters, answers your phone, and with whom you will probably have the most contact on a day to day basis. In many respects, your personal assistant is a more valuable team member than any lawyer, despite not usually having a charge-out rate.

First - please don't pick somebody too attractive. Whatever modern viewpoint you or others might hold, philandering with your support staff is still viewed as a highly questionable behaviour, and nothing will destroy your team faster. One simple way to avoid this is to remove any possibility of temptation. It's old fashioned, I know - but I am also right, and you know it.

The real issue is whether you should pick someone smart, or hard-working, or both. You see, a smart personal assistant is a great benefit - she can take initiative that you can trust, and she can offer ideas that will benefit you. The downside is that such assistants have a tendency to be short-term, because they frequently outgrow their positions and move on to greener pastures.

A hard-working assistant is similarly beneficial, but for different reasons. They will stay late with less complaint, work through lunch when required, and always "be there" when needed. The downside is that, over time, such assistants begin to realise that their wage is not commensurate with their hours. For internal parity, your assistant (no matter how talented) cannot necessarily be paid more than others, irrespective of her quality.

For my part, I believe you should pick smart over hard-working, but preferably both.

In doing so, accept the likelihood that your assistant will probably move on in time. In the meantime, develop the relationship, help her make the most of her time (and yours) and enjoy the benefits that come from having someone like that by your side. Then when she leaves, wish her well and start training the next one.

On to professional staff. This is more complicated.

Assuming the young lawyers around you will take a similar approach to practice that I have encouraged you to in times past, then you need to be wary.

The unfortunate truth is that, for a short time, you will have an opportunity to shape the young lawyers working for you - however, once that time ends, they will want to take your job. They will begin to hide things from you, they will start trying to develop professional relationships with your clients, and they will start to encroach on your practice.

If this sounds paranoid (and it probably does) then you also need to understand that I have seen this happen time and time again.

Lawyers are driven people, you see. Just like you are, and just like I am. We want more, and we rarely settle for too long in one station or with one set of responsibilities. As a result the young lawyers you hire will want to advance, and so you need to have an appreciation and understanding of that when it comes to building a team of professional staff around you.

You have a number of choices.

A common decision is to hire people young, get them while they are working hard, and to ensure that their long term prospects are so unclear that eventually they leave. This works particularly well with young lawyers in today's society, who seem to think that their career development should be handed to them on a silver platter.

I'm not sure that is necessarily the best approach, but it's certainly an option. There is no shortage of young lawyers around, and all of them will be keen for a time, so you can capitalise on that by using the most energy they are ever likely to have. You'll have a constant flow of young blood through the firm.

But the problem is succession. Over the longer term you need to develop at least a couple of the young lawyers around you to take over your role when you leave. I'm not sure if this is on your priority list, given the current role you have?

Either way, as a senior lawyer in your firm you have an obligation to be looking not just at the now, but also at the tomorrow, and the next week.

Part of that is not just clients, but also lawyers. Who will do your job when you leave? Will they do it as well as you do? Is there someone you can trust with your clients now, who will look after them in the future?

The legacy of a lawyer should be a longer one than just their immediate impact - it should take care of their firm and their clients long into the future.

That, Thomas, is why I suggest that even if you decide to avail yourself of naive young lawyers for the bulk of your work, you cultivate a couple of particularly talented young lawyers with a dedicated longer term succession plan. In doing this you are, of course, taking a risk. Your investment of time and money into their careers might be lost if they leave. But is it wasted? That depends on your perspective. It might be wasted in the sense that neither you nor your firm will get the benefit of the investment. However, the broader profession, those young lawyers, and their clients over the long term - these are the beneficiaries of your time, just as your firm and your clients are the beneficiaries of my investment into you.

In short, helping to develop young lawyers is a risk. But if you don't do that and they end up staying at your firm, then you might regret having left them to their own devices.

So what are you going to do? Also - let me know if this kind of letter is helping you, given I still don't really understand very well the nature of your current position. Perhaps you could take a minute to set it out for me?

Regards,

Uncle Andrew

ARE YOU MENTORING ANYONE?

Dear Thomas,

Thank you for clarifying a bit more about your position. I see that, for you at least, developing a team around you is not necessarily the highest priority you have at the moment although it might be relevant in some way.

Despite that, I wanted to touch on a topic that should be relevant - mentoring.

As you know, when I first started writing to you all those years ago, one of the things I mentioned was that I wanted to use my experience and expertise to help you in your career. Whatever your thoughts might be, my feeling is that I have offered to you a significant amount of guidance, information and wisdom gained from many years of practice.

Of course, I appreciate that throughout our time together you have not always agreed with me. Sometimes you have found me annoying, offensive, old fashioned or just plain wrong.

Naturally I was right and you were wrong (that was a joke, Thomas - don't get upset), but that is not the topic for today.

I wonder whether you have given any thought to doing the same? As I mentioned in my recent letter, there is certainly no shortage of young lawyers coming through the system. On almost a daily basis, the training offered to young lawyers becomes less and less relevant to actual legal practice.

We could, no doubt, express our frustration at this for many hours, but instead why not take an opportunity to make a difference, rather than simply complaining about the system?

There are many ways you can do this. I accept that I am old fashioned, and so the path than I took was one which was personal and relevant to me: I decided to mentor you.

Partly this was at the urging of your parents who, in their wisdom, convinced me that assisting in your professional development was a good use of my time and resources. As it turns out, they were right.

But the path I took need not be the path you should take. There are certainly many options today to make a difference in a young lawyers' life, not all of them requiring the kind of personal relationship that we developed.

Even within your own firm there are young lawyers wanting to build their confidence, develop their skills, start their networking and development, and raise the standard of legal practice in their own lives.

Doesn't that sound like something you could assist them with? Of course you are strapped for time, but how much time is really required in order to invest a little in the next generation?

At this point I feel it appropriate to revisit my thoughts on billable time.

When you were less senior, I recall writing to you with some thoughts about the importance of billable time, and what I suggested was that maximising your billable time should be at the forefront of your mind.

Over the last few years, I have had time to reflect on that advice. I still think it was correct.

At least, I still think it was correct for you, at that time, with the issues facing you at the time.

But is it correct for you now?

You see, over time you start not just to think it terms of cost and income, but also in terms of value. If you measure the value you provide purely by reference to your billable time or the bottom line, then you will become one dimensional.

At first, that was what you needed, but now you are starting to spread your wings (sorry for the poetry there) and you have far more to offer than sitting at your desk recording time.

You have experience.

You have knowledge.

You have wisdom.

And just as I have offered you pieces of those things over the years, you have an opportunity to do the same for those around you.

Is that what you are doing?

Best,

Uncle Andrew

Using Staff Properly

Thomas,

Now that you are in the process of building your team (acknowledging the limitations you have written to me about), we had also better discuss some concepts around how you are going to use them.

We've spoken about what kind of people you should be getting around you, and a little about mentoring, but we need to step back for a moment and consider what the point of all these human resources really is.

You'll recall that early in your career I explained to you that your job as a junior lawyer was to record as much billable time as humanly possible? Well - if you assume I would give your now junior staff the same advice (and I would) then you need to now consider how you fit into that equation.

Should you be billing as much as possible? Probably. But with your seniority you also need to be doing a number of other things to assist your team to reach its potential.

With a small team like yours, the situation need not be too complicated.

In short: you need to delegate things.

The question then really becomes: what should you delegate, and what should you not delegate. There is also a question about how to delegate properly that flows on once you have an idea of what you should keep in your own hands.

There is a prevailing view that work which can be done by someone more junior should be. But that poses a problem: if you hire a quality team as I have suggested, and if you are training them effectively, the point will swiftly arrive where there is no technical work at all that you will end up doing. While that might be nirvana for some lawyers, I expect that you (and the vast majority) became lawyers in the first place so you could actually practise law - not so you could help other people practise law around you.

There is also your ongoing career to consider, of course. The more you are out of the game, the less likely you will get the credit for a particular job, result or outcome. In fact what will begin to happen is that those working under you, despite having you to thank for your success, will likely start to take all the credit for your hard work.

So while I understand the proposition of pushing as much work down to lower level staff as possible, it really makes no sense to anyone who actually wants to practise law. If you delegate everything and end up doing nothing, you will find yourself resenting your time in the office.

The end result is that you need to retain some work that

demonstrates particular qualities. The first essential quality is that the client knows and trusts you. At this point you have a number of clients who appreciate your work already. They are less likely to make your life difficult, despite your increasing charge out.

Which leads to the second essential quality - the client needs to be able to afford you. You can see, I am sure, how this ties in closely with the first topic? Clients who trust you, and can afford you, are quite likely to pay your bills without complaint.

The final quality, perhaps less essential but certainly desirable - is that the work needs to be interesting to you. When you were junior this really didn't matter, but since you now have a chance to choose what work you do or don't do, why would you not keep that work which was the most interesting, stimulating or fascinating?

It can be a fine balance. On the one hand there are economic imperatives - if you do it right, you make more money by delegating to your young staff. They can deliver value quickly and effectively, for less cost to you and your firm.

On the other hand, you don't want to get bored in your career. You want to be a lawyer, after all - not a babysitter.

So find the balance that works for you - if you enjoy managing and do not mind losing some of your technical skills (it is not like riding a bike) then by all means delegate nearly everything. Provided you are using your remaining time by adding value of some sort, then there is no issue if all you do from day to day is develop relationship with clients and manage your team.

So what do you want to do?

All the best,

Andrew

MAKING MORE MONEY

Dear Thomas,

Making more money in your position now is very different from what it was before. In my time I earned a great deal of money, and I can assure you that it was not because I had any kind of peculiar talent in the law. What I do understand, however, is how a law firm functions. It wasn't too long ago you sought my guidance on how to stimulate some greater finances into your pocket - as I recall, it was not a successful endeavour.

You used to earn money - that is, you did your work, billed a lot, and were compensated accordingly through a salary. Now, however, your job is not really to earn money, but to make it. Your time is no longer dedicated entirely to file work, and your other responsibilities encroach - so your value to the firm has changed in character. In reality, the concept of earning "by the hour" should be absent from your thinking. As a result, to earn more money in your current position you need to know how your firm makes money, and where you fit in that puzzle.

Most firms, yours included, make money through a combination of three main factors: leverage, productivity, and revenue. Even though you have not chosen a partnership path, understanding these issues can offer you the ability to add significantly more value to your firm, and therefore earn considerably more money.

For a person of your experience now, revenue is pretty simple to understand - it's how much actual cash comes in the door.

But what about the rest? Just understanding revenue as you do is not understanding how the money flows through your firm, any more than enjoying eating icing is understanding how to bake a cake (the latter, for the record, is not something within my skill set, although the former certainly is).

By now I also expect that your understanding of productivity is quite established, or you would not have gotten as far as you have. No doubt you appreciate that the more that gets done, the more cash is generated? Of course, the productivity needs to be directed correctly, which is partly your role as both group leader and mentor. You need to ensure that the activities of your staff and colleagues are meaningfully dedicated towards the success of the firm, and not simply a series of random bumblings. Coordination here will allow productivity to soar, but a lacklustre approach to your guidance of the team effort will see you fall swiftly behind.

In terms of what to be productive on, to my mind your team needs to be focused on getting tasks out the door. Frequently I have seen groups with much activity, but little production. For you and where you are at, the more things that get finalised the better. For a start it causes a snow ball effect: people enjoy finishing things and getting the sense of accomplishment that comes with it - as a result, they work harder and faster on the next job to repeat the feeling that they get at the end of the first one. Over time, it becomes self-motivating.

On to leverage. Conceptually, leverage is quite simple: it's the process of creating more value for less cost.

There are some obvious examples: you delegate to junior staff who can do the job just as well. That frees you up to do more of what you should be doing, like marketing. Marketing is a higher value task, that cannot necessarily be done by more junior staff - as a result, if you are tied up on file work that could be done elsewhere, then the marketing simply does not get done.

Another example is dictation. I know it is becoming a little odd these days, but the reality is that dictation is faster, cheaper and more effective than you typing your own work. Of course you can type faster than I can, and so it becomes a more nuanced decision to make for each task. However, by the time you find an address, set up the document, write the letter, proof read it and then print it out - you are spending far more time than the few minutes it would take to dictate a letter. Thus, dictation is a form of leverage.

I am sure you get the point by now - anything you can do to accomplish the same task for less cost, should be your primary goal. This assumes, of course, that you have some higher value task to be getting on with. If you don't then that is a strategic issue.

I have found that a lot of lawyers around your level focus on file work because that is what they know - they do not have the confidence to actively engage in business development, and so immerse themselves in the comfort and relative safety of working on matters.

But now we must put these things together. You see, leverage allows you to lower the cost, productivity ensures that you maximise time spent on tasks, and revenue ensures that enough money is coming in the door.

All of these affect the profit that you and your team are yielding, and if one aspect is broken then you are missing a significant opportunity to add to the bottom line of the firm.

I have spent some time on this because it is critical if you are going to build your team that you understand how you need to be working in order to ensure profitability - do not just look at the money coming in the door, it is irrelevant how much revenue you generate. What is relevant is how much profit you generate.

I hope this has helped put the money in perspective.

The more value you add to your firm through understanding and implementing these principles, the more opportunity you will have to build up your team and spiral upwards in terms of your own income.

Best,

Uncle Andrew

TECHNOLOGY

Dear Thomas,

Despite what you might think (and your various jokes at my expense), I am not averse to using technology.

I am, however, averse to using technology badly.

Recently I wrote to you about leverage, and I think that in particular is where technology can be used to great advantage. Take, for example, the role of precedents.

When I was a junior lawyer the precedent was a document we started with but had to painstakingly copy out, word for word, in order to prepare a new document. They took a very different form to what they do now, because of course although we could copy things (within reason) the implementation of them was far less efficient than it can be now.

With electronic word processing, however, precedent documents have become a wonderful way of getting work done quickly and exercising leverage. IF (and it's a big if) you do it right.

The problem is the laziness that arises from precedents. I would be significantly more wealthy if I had a dollar for every time my question "why did you write this" was answered with "because it's in the precedent".

The existence of a phrase in a precedent is not a good enough reason for it to stay. It must have meaning, and it must have the right meaning. Otherwise it is fluff at best, and dangerous at worst.

So while I encourage you and your team to generate a bank of useful precedents to utilise as part of your profit system, I also espouse using it correctly. Recognise that a precedent is not a rule book, but merely a guideline. It frames the work, gives it its initial look and feel, but is not a set of handcuffs with which to bind your talent or that of your staff.

Also in the realms of helpful technology is dictation. I recognise that you and a number of your staff can probably type quite quickly, but I want to stress to you the importance of doing dictation and having someone expert type it. Although I wrote to you recently about this, I thought I would flesh it out a little in this letter since you so obviously disagreed with me.

Firstly, despite your ego the chances are extremely high that a professional typist will still type much faster than you.

Second, the time it takes to prepare a document is not simply the time it takes to type it. You have to get the file, identify the necessary elements (name, address, subject line etc) and you have get the formatting right. If you are doing a Court document you must ensure you are using the right form and have the correct headers. The list of periphery is quite extensive, and it is that which takes efficient production of a document out of the realms of the lawyer. If you save just 5 minutes on every document you produce, then dictation is absolutely worth it.

But think of dictation again as a form of leverage. It is a way of ensuring that you are reserved for necessary, high value work. Preparing documents, while important, can be done by less expensive staff and so you should definitely consider dictation to be part of your profit making arsenal.

I confess I am not up to date with everything that can be done, however, in terms of technology - what else is there that you can use these days to utilise technology as a form of leverage?

Best,

Andrew

ON SPECIALISATION

Dear Thomas,

As you approach your senior years as a legal practitioner I expect you will be looking to develop your practice within the confines of a specialist area. To become an expert beyond measure is indeed a worthy goal (although less important perhaps than being perceived as an expert).

The considerations here are many and varied, and I doubt I can give them all justice in this short letter.

I do, however, have some thoughts and will endeavour to share them with you as you consider the possibilities for your practice.

The first thing to be mindful of is this: the level of enjoyment you get from any given practice area is not a relevant consideration. I appreciate that you might like conveying property between individuals, but that is a fundamentally worthless area to specialise in.

Not because it doesn't need to be done, but because it's impossible to make enough money in the area to warrant the dedication it requires. You will find that, irrespective of your starting view of any area, if it is ultimately one which keeps you busy, valuable, and well paid – then you will come to like it enough to continue practising in the area.

That is just one example of course, I'm sure by now you realise that there are various practice areas amongst your colleagues where their specialisation is what could be charitably described as a mediocre endeavour. That is no criticism of them specifically, but rather an indication that they have, either through ignorance or conscious choice, decided upon a path that will ultimately be less beneficial for them.

For you, Thomas, the real money and viable future is going to be found in large scale investment banking work, mergers and acquisitions, or commercial litigation.

I have discounted personal injury law because, although potentially profitable, it frankly leaves a sour taste in my mouth. On the plaintiff side you will inexorably slide towards being an ambulance chaser. On the defendant side (for insurers, primarily) you will find that such companies put harsh limits upon what can be charged by their lawyers, and your fees and ultimate pay will be sacrificed as a result.

All personal matters may likewise be discounted. Wills, powers of attorney, conveyancing and the like are all best left to those content not to be earning much money.

Finally there are niche specialisations: healthcare law, internet law (whatever that is), sports law. None of these are, of course, actually an area of law at all, but are really just industries of focus. Anyone can turn their mind to those issues if required, so the benefit in limiting yourself to them is nonexistent.

I do not purport to deal with all possible iterations here, but only to highlight those which are most beneficial or otherwise for you.

Of course, the other reason I have selected those specialisations for you is the leverage you have through myself and your parents. We each have established contacts in those fields which, if asked in the right way, I am sure we can all use to assist you.

So what is it that you want to explore? You have enough decision making ability to get on with it now, and the seniority to start your specialisation - what's it to be?

Best,

Andrew

WHAT'S NEXT?

Dear Thomas,

I admit that we might be coming to the end of what I can offer you.

Your talents and your habits are now developed so that, if I ever had any influence over you at all, anything I can teach you is probably now going to fall into the category of "I knew that already".

It has been a fair journey, but I have found it distinctly satisfying - hopefully you have also.

So I have been spending some time thinking recently about where we might take ourselves next.

Do you have any thoughts? Do you feel like there is any remaining facet of what you need that I have yet to provide?

Of course, it is not that you have found out now everything that there is to know about legal practice and success in life. Far from it. Rather, it is simply that I have run out of wisdom to share with you, having such a limited supply to offer.

What I would like to encourage you to do therefore, is to ensure that you take what you know, weave it together, and keep asking yourself what is next.

There are any number of areas of your life and practice that we have not yet explored at all. I admit I took some umbrage to your personal choices earlier in your career, but of course beyond that we have never really touched on love and marriage? It may seem odd for an old man to offer any such advice, but of course it is a topic as large as any other, if not infinitely more complex.

We have yet to discuss (at all, as far as I can remember) any kind of spiritual pursuit. Have you found God (or has God found you)?

After all - I remain, as always, at your disposal.

Best,

Uncle Andrew

PART SIX
WHAT ON EARTH ARE YOU DOING?

Your Recent Announcement

Dear Thomas,

Over the years, I must admit that I have come to admire your resilience to a number of the principles that I endeavoured to teach you.

From the outset, I encouraged you (as I thought I should) to devote yourself fully and wholeheartedly towards success in your career. I hoped that, over time, I would provide you with some tools to do just that.

Recently I have come to regard you not as my junior, but rather as my esteemed colleague. In that spirit, our recent exchanges have (to me, at least) been those not of a mentor and student but rather a frank exchange of ideas and concepts between experienced professionals.

In hindsight I expect that some of my earlier tuition came across as overbearing, or sometimes judgemental. I trust you have regarded it over these years in the spirit that I intended it - a genuine attempt to help you in your own endeavours.

It is in that spirit that I have received your most recent update, where you have announced your retirement from the profession. In doing so, you become the youngest member of our family in history to retire from legal practice. You are not yet old enough to be ending your season of work, and not young enough to be making a foolhardy decision about your future (I recall computer games at one point entering your head as a valid way of making a living!)

I am divided.

On the one hand, my initial reaction was one of anger and dismay. I remember (some time ago now) writing to you about the obligations to your family that were your burden to carry. In doing so, I communicated to you not just my expectations, but those of your parents and the rest of the family.

Such a burden is not easily carried, and I know from our discussions and correspondence that there are many occasions on which you found this to be a chore. Yet, I had thought that over time you had become accustomed to legal practice and so I was shocked to hear of your departure from law. I was also more than a little surprised that you didn't discuss the decision with me before making it.

On the other hand, I cannot help but think that your move is more than a little inspiring. Frequently during the course of my own career I felt trapped. I was unable to extract myself from the profession and its trappings. You see, on the outside I was a successful, career oriented lawyer. But on the inside it was not uncommon for me to want something more in my life than simply my office, with its books and pomp.

And so, in that sense, you are making a transition that I could not. You are leaving the law, despite the pull that it has upon you, the money and power that it gives you, and the expertise you have gained over the years.

I cannot help but wonder this: what are you going to do?

Are you following a passion? Are you retiring in truth, and travelling the world? Do you have projects, ideas, businesses, books or charities in mind?

With your imminent freedom I imagine that you have spent a lot of time considering what you will do.

In my now more advanced years I am not in a position to enjoy whatever flexibility you have found for yourself, but nonetheless I can vividly imagine many options that I would have liked to pursue, had I grasped a chance to do so.

I look forward to hearing from you. Perhaps you might share your intentions with an old man?

Kind Regards,

Andrew

What's the Point of You?

Dear Thomas,

I realise that it hasn't been long since I last wrote, and so you have not had an opportunity to reply to me as yet.

However I wanted to write to you about a brief observation I have made about life since I, myself, retired. I thought that if I did so you might pick up some thoughts of interest or it might spark you to consider one thing or another.

You see, shortly after I retired I found myself with a problem. All through my time as a lawyer I had focused on being a lawyer. My conversations, studies, and goals are revolved around that single purpose.

Once I retired, of course, those things were redundant. I was left with very little to drive me each day.

It took me a considerable time to reconsider why I was here and what I should be doing. In short: I had no purpose.

Fortunately, although this is not a full time occupation I did have our correspondence. I had a number of small tasks that I wanted to accomplish, and so over time found myself with a renewed sense of vigour - but the journey to get there was not easy.

In reading more on the topic I have found that there are many others like me. Many who have defined themselves by reference only to their careers, rather than by reference to their humanity.

Although my accomplishments are many, at this point of my life they do seem a little hollow. That's not to suggest that what I did was unimportant - I think that I served many people well, and they benefited from my assistance. I just feel that gnawing sensation in my body that something was missing - or perhaps is still missing - from my life.

After all, although our careers are long lasting, they are rarely our entire lives. If they were intended to provide meaning, then our lives duration would only be the duration of our work - and after finishing, we would fade away.

So as you come to the end of your career, you might think not just about what you are going to do, but also why you are going to do it. What will drive you out of bed each morning with enthusiasm?

All the best,

Andrew

MORE ABOUT CHARITY

Dear Thomas,

It's wonderful to hear that you are finding avenues to use your skills, training and intelligence for the benefit of others.

There was a time (as you know too well) where I encouraged you to avoid charitable ventures. That was, I believe, what you needed at that stage of your career, and was advice I genuinely gave you to benefit your career.

But it is different now.

Perhaps I am becoming maudlin in my advanced years, but I find over time a more significant attraction towards the concept of giving back to the community which has treated me so well.

Unfortunately I am no longer in any position to take up those opportunities, but I am at least in a position to enjoy it when others do so.

You will find the board to which you are appointed to be a wonderful chance to use your talents.

But what about rest? Is your intended transition to this new venture one to start immediately, or would you begin with greater vigour after a short break to reflect upon life, the universe, and everything.

Your wife and young children would no doubt enjoy a short trip. If, as a friend, I can offer some advice to you in this transition it is this: do not neglect those who love you unconditionally.

When I lost my wife, one of the things that hit me immediately was a feeling of profound regret. Even thinking of it now the emotions are quite raw.

For a lawyer, as I am sure you know, emotional response is not necessarily the first response to a given stimulus. But, despite appearances, I know (as you do) that our clinical exterior is not always a reflection of our true reaction.

So I do suggest you take a moment. Think about your work to date, and the toll that it has taken on your family and your self.

Perhaps with a few minutes contemplation you might want to avail yourself of a short sojourn to Europe or the Islands?

It's up to you, of course. But before leaping into the fray, enjoy what you have, while you still have it.

In making this recommendation it comes from a genuine hope that you never have to experience regret as a result of your diligence, as I have.

I look forward to hearing from you.

Best,

Andrew

PS - I joined Facebook recently - did you get my "friend request"?

CATCHING UP

Dear Thomas,

With all our correspondence over the years, it has not been often that we have been able to catch up in person, so I was very happy when you stopped by recently.

What I noticed almost immediately was the energy with which you came up the stairs and entered the room. Your eyes were bright and your demeanour was confident and relaxed.

What our conversation brought me was a much better understanding of just how fulfilling you are finding your role now, and how much delight it is bringing to you and to your family.

With that, I must admit that after you left I spent a lot of time dwelling on my own life, and the contributions that I have made to others, to society, and to my family.

I also spent some time thinking about what I sacrificed to take the path that I did.

There are days now when I still believe that the sacrifices I made were worthwhile. Missing family events, being absent from my wife for extended periods, and spending a great deal more time with my colleagues than my friends.

However, there are other days when I cannot help but wonder if all of that was really worth it. I see what you are doing now, and I see the amount of life that it has injected into you, and I speculate that perhaps there was a better path.

Perhaps it is a function of modern society that such opportunities exist? As much as you might think me stuck into a tiny pigeon hole, you must also remember that when I was growing up, training and practising in the law, everything was very different. Professions and careers looked far more linear then than they do now. The options once I became a legal practitioner were effectively limited to continuing that practice.

You, however, have shown me that with enough chutzpah you can, in fact, take a different direction to that which the masses take, and do so successfully and meaningfully.

In that, despite my pushing for a very different approach in your life, I can only hope that at least some of the decisions you have made have been impacted positively by my letters, advice and assistance over the years.

Returning to where I started - thinking about the contribution I have made, I cannot help but think (if you will indulge me) that of all the matters I worked on, advices I gave, bills I issued - they pale in comparison to the success that I have had in helping you become the man that you have.

It is a comforting thought for me.

Signing off,

Andrew

PART SEVEN
REFLECTIONS FROM THOMAS

MY TIME WITH ANDREW

[Editor's Note - although I did not manage to locate Thomas' responses to Uncle Andrew through the years, I did manage to get Thomas himself to contribute a few thoughts about his time with Uncle Andrew.]

Thanks for asking about my mentoring by Uncle Andrew. It's always interesting to reflect on the events and people that have shaped us.

On the one hand, I have a family of overachievers. They are smart, dedicated and hard working. In that respect they are worthy of respect and emulation.

Of course, there is the pressure. High grades, top firms, long hours, and early elevation in their fields. If you are a child in such a family, how are you supposed to live up to that history?

Naturally I wanted to go with the flow. I wanted to copy my parents, see their success, and to live up to the standards expected of me.

When Uncle Andrew offered his help, I was actually very glad for it. I didn't know him that well (aside from the occasional family get-together) and I really didn't know what to expect.

Obviously, through university, I ignored most of what he had to say (I doubt I kept many of his "helpful" letters during that period at all, to be honest).

When I hit the profession, that's really when he went into overdrive though.

I know that Uncle Andrew was successful. He'd built a firm, gotten far, and had some great clients. But he actually never quite managed to realise that my heart wasn't in it. I suspect, given some of his comments, that he did in fact understand me better deep down then he indicated on his prickly surface. I did try to engage with him, to see if he could help me love the profession more, but in fact I just didn't quite get it.

It took me a while to realise that, of course. I told myself that over time things would start to get better, that I'd fit in more with the people around me who didn't seem to mind their lives revolving around the office.

It never really happened. I didn't hate my job. But I didn't love it either.

If you've seen Uncle Andrew's letters, you've probably noticed that I annoyed him a bit sometimes. Sure, I did OK at my job - I just didn't really like it that much. I wasn't invested enough, and eventually I decided to bail.

To be honest, Andrew took it fairly well - far better than I had expected him to. I didn't want to tell him in advance about my decision, because I would have received a ream of paper about it from him, but as it turns out he must have mellowed a bit.

I learnt a lot from Andrew. He actually did teach me how to survive in the office, even if some of his ideas were a little off at times.

His thoughts on marketing, networking and building relationships came from a great place. Of course, he couldn't get his head into anything other than football as a chance to hob nob with people, but that's OK - he liked football.

Andrew had a lot to offer young lawyers. I've come to realise that the way I learnt from him is the same as any mentor really - there is always a lot of advice, many suggestions, gratuitous opinions and insight - but ultimately what you have to do is "eat the fish, and throw out the bones".

If you are a young lawyer and for some reason you are reading this, then I'd encourage you to do something similar.

That's all I've got, really.

Signing out,

Thomas.

PART EIGHT
ABOUT THE AUTHOR

I'M JUST... ME

Hi there - I'm Chris.

I've been working in law firms since 2001, and a lawyer since 2005. Of course, that means I'm old-ish, but not so old that I've forgotten what it feels like to be a young lawyer, new to practice, and new to working with other people in a high pace environment.

In 2013 I started Tips for Lawyers, which was fundamentally designed to be a platform to sell my first book: Look Before you Leap.

You see, although I'd written a book I didn't really know what to do with it, or how to get it in front of people. Things have come a long way since then.

I've been learning many new skills, a lot of which don't exactly come naturally to someone who did a law degree. However, with some perseverance and a lot of mistakes, I've managed to build up www.tipsforlawyers.com to a successful venture, helping tens of thousands of young lawyers along the way to explore issues, learn skills, and build their confidence.

I hope you've enjoyed this book. I wanted to do something a bit different, and with any luck that's what I've achieved.

The inspiration for this book came from C.S Lewis' book called "The Screwtape Letters", where Lewis provides one side of a dialogue designed to teach us some fundamental truths about the nature of God and the nature of the enemy.

Legal careers can be hard. That said, I've tried to approach the information here with a certain amount of mild humour. I gave Uncle Andrew a few opinions that probably aren't politically correct, but thankfully that is the protection we get when we rely upon fictional characters in our writing.

I'm all over the internet, and so I hope you'll reach out and say hello. The best place to do it is at www.tipsforlawyers.com, where I hope you've registered for one of the free courses that I mentioned in the first chapter.

You can also find me to say hello:

- on twitter, @joyouslawyer
- on LinkedIn, https://www.linkedin.com/in/hargreaveschris

So for now, signing off - thanks again for your support in buying this, and thanks for the positive review I'll hope you leave.

Happy Lawyering!

<<<<THE END>>>>